Making the
MOST
of Your CORE
READING
Program

Peter Dewitz • Jonni Wolskee

Making the
MOST
of Your CORE
READING
Program

Research-Based Essentials

HEINEMANN
Portsmouth, NH

Heinemann
361 Hanover Street
Portsmouth, NH 03801–3912
www.heinemann.com

Offices and agents throughout the world

The authors and publisher wish to thank those who have generously given permission to reprint borrowed material:

Excerpt from *Alexander and the Wind-Up Mouse* by Leo Lionni. Copyright © 1969, copyright renewed 1997 by Leo Lionni. Used by permission of Alfred A. Knopf, an imprint of Random House Children's Books, a division of Random House, Inc. Used by permission of the publisher and the Author's estate.

Figure 3.4: Excerpt from *Hold the Anchovies!* by Shelley Rotner and Julia Pemberton Hellums. Text copyright © 1996 by Shelley Rotner and Julia Pemberton Hellums. Used by permission of Orchard Books, an imprint of Scholastic Inc.

Acknowledgments for borrowed material continue on p. x.

Cataloging-in-Publication data is on file with the Library of Congress.

Editor: Tobey Antao
Development editor: Kerri Herlihy
Production: Vicki Kasabian
Cover and interior designer: Monica Ann Crigler
Typesetter: Publishers' Design & Publishing Services, Inc.
Manufacturing: Steve Bernier

Printed in the United States of America on acid-free paper
16   15   14   13   12   ML   1   2   3   4   5

From Peter
To my loving wife Pamela,
who put up with endless boring weekends while I wrote this book
and who encourages me in all I do.

● ●

From Jonni
To my loving family:
Thank you for all your love and support,
with special thanks to my mom Patti
for her many words of encouragement.
I love you.

To Deb:
Twelve years ago you were my mentor;
twelve years later you continue to be my very good friend and confidante.
Thank you for everything.

To my many wonderful friends:
Thank you for enabling me to keep my sanity and never failing to make me laugh.
Love you Stephanie, Amie, Cary, Mandy, Kim, Jen, Jamie, Sarah, and Stacy.

Contents

Acknowledgments   xi

Introduction   xiii

1. Get to Know Your Core Reading Program, Again!   1

The core reading program approach to reading instruction   2

A brief history of core reading programs   3

How a core reading program is created   8

Are core reading programs built on reading research?   10

How should reading be taught?   11

Extending your learning   12

Further reading   12

2. Think Beyond Your Core Reading Program's Five-Day Lesson Plan   13

What research says about how teachers use reading programs   14

The planning guides in your core reading program   14

Beginning the school year   15

Setting goals for your students   17

Allocating time for reading instruction   20

Planning a unit of instruction with your core program   22

Planning a week of instruction with your core program   28

Planning assessments   36

Extending your learning   39

What Does the Research Say About How Children Acquire Independent Word Reading Skills?   42

How do children learn to read?   42

Why is phonemic awareness critical to learning to read?   43

Why is direct instruction in phonics essential for most students?   44

Will instruction and drill on phonics patterns lead to accurate and fluent word recognition?   45

What kinds of books support learning to read?   46

Should young readers be encouraged to use context and pictures to identify words?   46

Why do some children struggle with learning to read?   47

Do all children need the same type of reading instruction?   47

3. Fine-Tune the Whole-Group Lessons in Your Core Reading Program   49

Whole-group instruction in your core reading program   49

What research says about whole- and small-group instruction   50

Activities that can and should take place in whole-group instruction   51

Extending your learning   70

Further reading   70

4. Enhance Your Core's Word Study Program   73

Word study in your core reading program   74

What research says about word study   75

Organizing your small groups   75

Sequencing phonemic awareness and phonics instruction   77

Coaching students to apply word recognition strategies   84

Teaching high-frequency words to all students   87

Word study for struggling readers   89

Word study for English language learners   90

Independent work for all readers   91

Summing it up   95

Extending your learning   95

Further reading   96

5. Add Independent Reading and Small-Group Intervention to Build Fluency   97

Fluency instruction in your core reading program   98

What research says about how children become fluent readers   99

The first road to fluency: Independent reading   100

Structuring independent reading with book clubs   104

Structuring independent reading with literature circles   106

The second road to fluency: Teacher-guided practice   107

Fluency-oriented reading instruction   110

Extending your learning   111

Further reading   112

What Does the Research Say About the Development and Teaching of Reading Comprehension?   113

How do readers comprehend?   113

How does comprehension ability develop in children?   115

What is the difference between a comprehension skill and a comprehension strategy?   116

How many strategies do children need to be taught?   116

How should skills/strategies be taught?   117

How can growth in comprehension be assessed?   118

6. Boost Your Core Reading Program's Vocabulary Instruction   120

Vocabulary instruction in your core reading program   122

What research says about vocabulary instruction   123

Word-learning tasks   124

Selecting words to teach   127

Teaching for retention   132

Word-learning strategies   135

Activities that foster word consciousness   136

Extending your learning   138

Further reading   138

7. Build Knowledge to Increase Understanding   140

Knowledge and comprehension instruction in your core reading program   141

What research says about building knowledge in comprehension instruction   142

Creating units that build knowledge   143

Techniques for activating prior knowledge   151

Techniques for building new knowledge   154

Extending your learning   155

Further reading   156

8. Develop Comprehension in Small Groups   157

Small-group comprehension instruction in your core reading program   159

What research says about small-group comprehension instruction   160

Planning your guided comprehension lessons   160

Teaching your guided comprehension lessons   163

Differentiating your comprehension instruction   170

Extending your learning   176

Further reading   176

References   177

Acknowledgments

I would like to thank the many teachers and administrators in the Accomack County Schools and other districts around the country who helped shape my thinking about teaching reading and encouraged the love of reading. Specifically I took inspiration from Adam Hopkins, Kim Graham, Deonne Beckwith, Rick Ingram, Lara Wallace, Christina Whayland, Linda Boswell, Joan Doughty, Megan Fenwick, Nora Laaksonen, Emily Roehn, and Wendy Roache.

– Peter

I would like to acknowledge my Capital School District family. I am a product of this district, and it gave me great pleasure to return here to begin my teaching career. During my time at Capital, I have had the privilege to work with many talented colleagues and administrators who have had a huge impact on how I teach in the classroom today. It is my hope that the Capital community is as proud of this book as I am of them.

– Jonni

We would like to thank the many individuals at Heinemann who helped make this book possible: Margaret LaRaia, who recognized the value of our ideas; Tobey Antao and Kerry Herlihy, who edited this book carefully, provided enlightening feedback, and taught us how to write; Vicki Kasabian, who guided this book and us through the production process; Alan Huisman who edited it, and Eric Chalek, who kept his steady hand on marketing the book and who knows, along with John Steinbeck, the true reason to write.

– Peter & Jonni

Introduction

If you have picked up this book, you are most likely using a core reading program. You may work in a school where you must use the core program as written, remaining faithful to it, or you may have the freedom to pick and choose your way through it. If you are being faithful to the program, you might have noticed that the needs of strong readers or struggling readers are not being met. If you are using the program selectively, you might want more insight about the structure of core programs and the characteristics of their materials and lessons. This book is for all teachers who wish they could reach *every* reader but feel their program can't stretch that far. You are not alone. In fact, we've written this book because so many teachers want to do better but find that they butt up against the limitations of their reading program.

It's like the family that outgrows its house but isn't in a position to buy a new one. Adding on can solve the problem without incurring the expense of a new home. New core programs are expensive, and in tight monetary times remodeling is less expensive. If your school has the resources and the knowledge to teach reading with existing materials, *Making the Most of Your Core Reading Program* is the blueprint for remodeling that core program—adding helpful ways to support every student. You know the work will be done well because you're doing it, and we're certain you'll be happy with the outcome because the blueprint calls for a strong foundation of theory and research and extra-thick studs reinforced by successful classroom experiences. In many cases the research that has led to the ideas we share is deeper, more current, and more balanced than that which builds the foundation of core reading programs!

While modifying instruction may seem like extra work, these instructional strategies are well worth your and your students' time. Responding to instructional needs that commonly crop up with core programs or in many classrooms, our book helps you:

- Increase flexibility in lesson planning.
- Ensure that whole-group lessons reach all students.
- Differentiate word study through small-group instruction.
- Make space for independent reading to build fluency, knowledge, and enthusiasm.
- Boost vocabulary instruction.

- Deepen and broaden readers' prior knowledge.
- Support comprehension and thinking via small-group instruction.

This list may suggest some of the reasons that struggling readers aren't always well supported by core programs (McGill-Franzen et al. 2006). It may also suggest why we believe *Making the Most of Your Core Reading Program* can bring hope to those students and their teachers.

No matter the context in which you teach, we firmly believe, as do many researchers, that the teacher is the key to successful reading instruction—not the materials that come in the box (Bond and Dykstra 1967; Allington 2009). It's the person who opens the box that matters most. We decided to write this book because we believe our knowledge, experience, and instructional recommendations can help you and your school use the materials in your core reading program better with little added expense or wasted time and effort.

Why are we so sure we can support you? Peter is a researcher, professor, and staff developer who has worked with many public schools, especially schools that were part of the federal Reading First program. Doing this work, he came to understand that following a core reading program with fidelity usually shortchanges struggling readers, bores the best readers, and often turns reading instruction into a mind-numbing routine for everyone. Peter's published research substantiates that belief, especially for comprehension instruction (Dewitz, Jones, and Leahy 2009). Jonni, a very successful kindergarten/first-grade teacher and reading specialist, brings years of experience to our work. A veteran of core reading programs, she knows when to follow the program, when to modify it, and even when to ignore it. Our goal is to share knowledge and insight about core reading programs that can help you feel more confident about making decisions that will benefit your students. We want you to think of the core reading program as a toolbox and us as guides to using its tools most effectively and knowing when you must go beyond that toolbox to meet the needs of your students.

We begin by looking at a core reading program from the publisher's viewpoint to see how the materials get there in the first place and why the developers of a core program want you to teach reading in a certain way. We then present a brief history of reading programs to show you how the program you are using today incorporates instructional practices that are decades old. Finally, we present our view on how core programs can be used most effectively. Obviously, we think they may not be comprehensive enough to help every reader, so we share proven instructional ideas that can bolster the effectiveness of any reading program. By understanding the instructional design of a core reading program, you'll be able to make more effective decisions in your classroom, and you'll know how to add the exciting instructional practices we recommend. Along the way you'll find sample lessons plans, planning guides, instructional strategies, ways to extend your understanding, and other helpful supports that are great for individual practitioners and even better for teams or whole schools.

Helping children become lifelong readers is everyone's ultimate goal, but many children need more than a core reading program can offer. Our book puts a few more tools in your toolbox to help you give every single reader you teach a shot not just at proficiency but at a lifetime love of reading.

CHAPTER 1

Get to Know Your Core Reading Program, Again!

For most of their existence core reading programs were called *basals*. The term *basal* meant base or foundation of reading instruction. From that base the teacher could modify or add to the foundation, crafting a reading program that met the diverse needs and interests of her students. With the switch in terminology to *core* came the assumption that the program was vital and necessary. All reading instruction revolved around or was tied to this essential core. Many advocated that these core programs should be followed faithfully. Throughout this book we will call these programs *core reading programs*, but we view them as basals and therefore agree with Arthur Gates, one of the creators of the modern reading program:

> I have always believed that if one accepts the theory that the basal reading program must be used it should be adjusted to individual needs and that each child should be encouraged to move on into wider and more advanced material as rapidly as possible. [cited in Smith 1986, 224]

A core reading program includes the content and methods for teaching reading. The content is the reading selections and leveled books provided for the students. The methods are the units, lessons, worksheets, and assessments that help teachers make instructional decisions. Core reading programs have been with us for generations, and with each passing decade they have become more comprehensive and more complex. The teacher's manual for the *Stickney Primer* published by Ginn and Company in 1885 included just five pages of teaching suggestions. Almost one hundred years later the teacher's manual for just the primer volume of Ginn's Reading 720 Rainbow program (1980) was 316 pages long.

In the newest core reading program, *Journeys*, published by Houghton Mifflin Harcourt, the first of six volumes of the first-grade teacher's edition is 672 pages long. The complexity of these programs cries out for teachers to make astute decisions in meeting the needs of their students and leading them to the wider world of children's literature and nonfiction inquiry.

Each company that publishes a core reading program has a culture and history of reading instruction. These folks have created reading materials for decades and have confidence in their know-how. The program you are using today likely incorporates instructional practices that date back decades. We want you to understand how these publishers think and what goes into the process of creating a core reading program. Once you understand the development process and the thinking of the publishers you will also understand the limits of the programs and why they should not carry the research-based stamp. They are useful tools, but the research-based label gives them a degree of power they do not deserve. Understanding the instructional design of a core reading program will help you make effective decisions in the classroom and incorporate new and exciting instructional practices not currently part of a basal program.

THIS CHAPTER WILL HELP YOU:
- Understand the history of core reading programs.
- Appreciate that the process of creating a core reading program involves principles of reading research and sales marketing.
- Question the claim that core reading programs are research-based.
- Embrace the importance of using the programs in ways that will meet the needs of your students.

The Core Reading Program Approach to Reading Instruction

As most of us know from experience, a core reading program presents a well-structured routine for teaching reading, and teachers are expected to follow it. In the typical classroom, the teacher introduces and reviews skills in a daily whole-group session and perhaps reads a selection aloud, and the students read the related selection in the anthology with a page-by-page discussion led by the teacher. Then the class is typically split into three small groups, and each group reads a leveled book with teacher guidance. When groups are not working with the teacher, they complete workbooks and worksheets, sometimes at their desk, other times at learning centers. (A learning center is often nothing more than a workbook disassembled and moved to a corner of the room.) These instructional routines remain virtually unchanged from September through May and from first grade through fifth grade. The conventional wisdom is that by following this routine the students will progress in reading ability. Most do.

But does this routine serve the students from poor backgrounds who struggle with literacy, often with little support at home, or those who find learning to read a breeze? Does it excite and enhance the literacy skills of children who are already competent readers? Does it create avid readers? Unfortunately, the answer is a resounding no.

Underlying all core reading programs is the belief that learning to read is about acquiring skills—decoding, fluency, vocabulary, and comprehension skills (Barr and Sadow 1989; Chambliss and Calfee 1998). Learn enough skills and you will become a good reader. So reading instruction becomes a series of skills lessons, filled with workbooks to practice skills and the reading of short texts in which teachers question students on their use of these skills (Durkin 1979; Dewitz, Jones, and Leahy 2009). But becoming literate also requires knowledge and motivation. Good readers are knowledgeable, use that knowledge to comprehend what they read, and thus build more knowledge, whether of concepts like history or ecology or of the interpersonal forces that drive our lives. Core reading programs do little to build knowledge (Walsh 2003; Hirsch 2011).

Reading is also motivated behavior. Readers read all the time, for pleasure, for information, for escape, and while text messaging. When you say that someone is a reader you are making a broad statement about her behavior, her desire to read, her motivation. The concept of reading contains within it the attribute of motivation. Reading must be willed. Reading requires choice. At times reading is difficult and you must persevere. There is little about the routine in core reading programs that builds a deep desire to read. At best most core programs incorporate some gamelike activities, teachers read aloud to students, and the better readers can deviate from the routine to read novels and other trade books.

A core reading program is also built on the assumption that all the materials you need to teach reading come in the box and that you must use the materials. This assumption can lead to the reading of dull and unnecessary stories. It can cause teachers to give workbook assignments that are unnecessary and ask students to practice activities they do not need. Since the school district pays for these programs, teachers feel compelled to follow the program rather than try other activities and materials that could enhance a student's daily reading experience.

A Brief History of Core Reading Programs

For over three hundred years teachers have believed that young children needed special books to learn to read. The young child cannot read what the adult does, so educators wrote easier books with shorter stories, easier words, and lots of repetition. Educators have never agreed about the content and wording of these books, and the disagreements continue today. The history of basal readers is actually the history of American reading instruction, and it has been chronicled many times over the decades. The most important work is *American Reading Instruction*, by Nila Banton Smith, first published in 1965 and updated in 1986. All other histories derive from this book, including the brief one in *The Essential Guide to Selecting and Using Core Reading Programs* (Dewitz et al. 2010), which is the first to describe the contemporary era.

The first reading books for children coincide with the founding of the nation in the late eighteenth century. Starting about 1774 the *New England Primer* was the dominant tool for teaching young children to read and was widely used until 1830 (Chall and Squire 1991). Its competition was the *American Spelling Book* created by Noah Webster in 1788. It was soon apparent that one book was not sufficient for teaching reading, and educators and publishers began to develop a series of reading books, one for each grade. The most dominant were the McGuffey Eclectic Readers published from 1836 to 1920, with over 120 million copies in print (Chall and Squire 1991). This is a key point; basals, as they were known at the time, were always created by educators working with private business. They have never been nor are they now purely research-based materials.

1920s to 1960s: Dick and Jane, Janet and Mark

By the 1920s and 1930s the modern basal reader had begun to take shape. The most widely used series was Dick and Jane, first called the Elson Readers (1910 to 1936); then the Basic Readers, by Gray and Arbuthnot (1940–1948); and finally the Curriculum Foundation series until its demise in the mid-1960s. It is estimated that over 200 million children learned to read with Dick and Jane (Chall and Squire 1991) published by Scott Foresman, now a part of the Pearson publishing conglomerate. The Dick and Jane series and its many competitors introduced many characteristics found in today's core reading programs.

The Dick and Jane books started with a primer, then a first reader, second reader, up through the sixth grade. Later a "preprimer" was added to the series. In the 1920s the teacher's edition was added, first a very slim addendum to the pupils' book and then a stand-alone volume. At first the teacher's edition contained just a few teaching suggestions, plus answers to the questions in the pupils' edition. Gradually it began to grow, and by the late 1960s the first-grade teacher's edition numbered over 300 pages, still short compared with the multivolume teacher editions in today's core programs. (Does the increasing length of the teacher's manual imply a mistrust of the teacher or the need to script them?)

The Dick and Jane program and its competitors also introduced the first workbooks in which children matched pictures to pictures, matched words and sentences to pictures, and spelled words. The publishers labeled these activities *initial sound matching*, *vocabulary*, *drawing conclusions*, and so forth. Early on the publishers used eye-catching labels to highlight important skills, without necessarily creating rich or effective instruction (Durkin 1981).

The reading instruction in Dick and Jane centered on a few core ideas. Beginning reading instruction stressed a whole word approach. Students were introduced to sight words, and these words were repeated frequently within and across stories. It was the constant repetition of these words that gave the stories their distinctive voice: "Go, Jane. Go, Jane, go." Phonics instruction was not absent from these programs, but it was not the focus. Phonics was built into the workbooks. At the beginning of each lesson the teacher introduced the words for the week. The students read the stories while the teacher asked comprehension questions, and the discussion continued after the students finished. This basic plan of introducing words, then a page-by-page guided comprehension lesson, followed by postreading discussion continues with little variation to this day.

1970s–1980s: A Shift to Skills

The basals of this era reflected the growing view that learning to read demanded the mastery of numerous reading skills, the focus being phonics and comprehension. Publishers beefed up the skills instruction in their programs, added skills lessons to the teacher's manual, provided more workbooks and reteaching worksheets. The package was tied together by a skills management system, a series of pretests and posttests used to identify the needs of individual students and track their mastery of each individual skill (Johnson and Pearson 1976). These new components did not replace but were added to the older routine of reading the basal story, answering the guided reading questions, and conducting the postreading discussion. The new skills lessons were typically short, with minimal explanation, and focused more on practicing and assessing skills than on providing explicit instruction (Durkin 1981). Modeling and thinking aloud were not yet attributes of basal reading programs. Reading instruction became more complex, and reading programs too become more complex. Teachers were offered more options. More assessments were added, along with additional workbooks, big books, spelling books, and writing instruction.

The latter part of this era also brought a new focus on reading comprehension. In the mid-1970s, researchers at the Center for the Study of Reading (CSR) turned their attention to understanding the process of reading comprehension (Anderson and Pearson 1984, for example), and from that work many new instructional ideas emerged, the most important being a strong focus on using prior knowledge and creating strategic readers. Instructional ideas like story mapping, understanding expository text structure, graphic organizers, and metacognition all trace their roots to CSR (Dole et al. 1991). These new ideas, especially comprehension strategies, eventually made their way into the basal reading programs and took their place alongside the comprehension skills already present. Teacher-directed lessons became more explicit; teachers were encouraged to model and think aloud and become more precise in their guided practice.

1990s: Whole Language and Literature-Based Instruction

The heavy focus on skills stemming from new philosophies of reading instruction eventually brought a change to basal readers. Whole language rejected the piecemeal skills approach to reading instruction in favor of starting with real texts read for real purposes. Whole language educators encouraged teachers to help students with skills as needed but to avoid following a rigid scope and sequence of instruction. Literature-based instruction rejected the controlled vocabulary text that had been the mainstay of basals for decades, and the developers of basal readers constructed the pupils' edition from children's literature originally written for children and parents. Since vocabulary was no longer controlled, reading got harder for the youngest students (Hoffman et al. 1994). Students in first grade had to learn more, generally harder words, and each word was repeated less often compared with older programs. Building a vocabulary became more difficult.

With the move toward "authentic" text, the emphasis on skills and strategies declined. Phonics was still present in the programs, but the instruction was less explicit than it would be again ten years later. The approach to comprehension skills and strategies was softened by the inclusion of response to literature and book clubs. Even these new initiatives were not as robust as their original developers intended (see McMahon and Raphael 1997/2007). These changes in basal programs were not extreme. The core structure of the programs remained the same. Students were introduced to skills and read a story each week while their teacher asked guided questions and led a postreading discussion. Basal reading programs do not undergo wholesale change; rather, instructional elements are added, some are deleted, and others diminished or highlighted.

2000 to the Present: A Balanced Literacy Approach

The most recent movement in reading instruction carries the label of *balanced literacy*, and describing what is being balanced requires some background. At least two forces influenced the shape or structure of today's core reading programs.

First, the National Reading Panel report in 2000 emphasized five critical components of reading—phonemic awareness, phonics, fluency, vocabulary, and comprehension—and any program that wanted to remain viable had to include these components in its design. So phonics instruction was reemphasized, along with phonemic awareness. Activities to develop fluency were added, since these had not been a focus in previous programs. These programs were critically evaluated by review panels and given the label *scientifically based reading research*, and publishers stressed this fact when they sold their programs (Simmons and Kame'enui 2003). The programs were also rebranded as core reading programs to reflect their central critical place in reading instruction.

The second influence on the shape of current programs stemmed from both the guided reading approach (Fountas and Pinnell 1996) and the growing realization that one text, at one reading level, does not meet the needs of all students. All of the publishers responded by adding leveled "little books" to their reading programs. Now children read the basic anthology story—interesting children's literature—early in the week and then later read a little leveled book aimed at students who are reading above grade level, on grade level, or below grade level or are English language learners. Most programs have also added a set of decodable books to assist with phonics instruction in kindergarten and first and second grade (Adams 2009).

Introducing leveled books was the first serious attempt publishers made to differentiate instruction. Prior to that the programs handled differentiation through reteaching activities (typically more worksheets for students who tested poorly on individual skills) and occasional instructional hints to teachers to modify the instruction for special groups (English language learners and struggling readers). The latest editions of core reading programs contain small-group lessons for students reading above, on, and below grade level. They provide lessons for small-group instruction but still keep the whole-group focus that had dominated basals for decades. In some programs the instructional lessons for a below-grade-level reader differ from the lessons for an above-grade-level reader. In other programs the leveled book changes but the instruction does not.

This brief history documents two important facts. First, reading programs have not changed radically over the decades. The basic structure of the lesson has remained the same.

Students still read stories under the teacher's guidance. Skill instruction has steadily increased, but the texts that students read have changed to accommodate literature-based instruction, guided reading, and need for decodable texts. There is an overall trend toward more differentiated instruction, although some publishers have pursued this more aggressively than others. Second, a core reading program is one framework for teaching reading, guided reading is another (Fountas and Pinnell 1996). A core reading program is an eclectic framework that merges the guided reading of short texts with skills instruction. It is consistently a teacher-directed activity in which little responsibility is given to the students to develop their own skills and their own initiative. It favors a strict instructional routine that supports the teaching and practice of skills over the development of knowledge or motivation.

How a Core Reading Program Is Created

It is difficult to describe fully the process of developing a basal reader, especially if you are not an author, an editor, or a publisher. Peter was on the author team of Literature Works, a core reading program published by Silver Burdett Ginn in 1997. In 2009 he interviewed authors, publishers, and editors from the major companies that develop core reading programs. The results of these interviews first appeared in *The Essential Guide to Selecting and Using Core Reading Programs* (Dewitz et al. 2010) and are summarized below.

The title page of every teacher's edition lists the authors of the program. These educators/researchers do not write the program. They are consultants and advisors to the publishers; they attend meetings, guide the development of the materials, review materials, speak on behalf of the reading program, and receive royalties for their work. The development of a core reading program is far more complex than lone authors working behind computers writing lessons and creating instructional materials. Creating a core reading program requires the work of editors, authors, graphic designers, and marketing experts at a major publishing house. It also requires the efforts of editors, writers, and graphic designers at development houses—educational support services who do much of the real work. Finally, many freelance writers are commissioned to create the 500-plus leveled little books and the myriad of workbook activities that are part of any core reading program.

The creation of any core program really begins in the state departments of education, particularly California, Texas, and Florida, who prescribe the skills that must be taught and outline the shape of the instruction. For publishers to succeed financially they must adhere to these state guidelines. Next, the publisher must define the new program's important characteristics. Will it emphasize phonics, comprehension, exciting vital texts, or differentiated instruction? What is the program's message? To reach this decision the publisher, editors, marketing executives, and authors must consider the current and future trends in reading instruction, findings from research, national policy (like the 2000 National Reading Panel Report), and what schools want. What are the new components of the program—a new manual for teaching English language learners? fold-up learning centers? Core reading programs are first and foremost market driven; they must make money to thrive.

Next, authors, editors, and marketing experts design the program. They begin with the weekly lesson plan—the essential structuring element. This is a collaborative effort; together they explore ideas and create and revise prototype lessons until consensus is reached. They consider the elements of the lesson plan (morning message, skills lesson, during-reading questions, postreading discussion or personal response to literature), the sequence of the instructional ideas (should the skills be taught before or after the story is read?), and what the teacher should say at each point in the lesson to support and assess students' understanding, direct thinking, and provide feedback. Teachers, in a focus group, then review the prototype lessons. The goal of the focus group is to voice an opinion about which lesson plan design and which lesson elements teachers desire. From our interviews and research we learned that this market research is more important to the publisher than "scientifically based reading research" because the program must sell (Dewitz et al. 2010). The program authors are important voices in the room but not the only voices.

Once the lesson plan is created, the literature must be selected and the hundreds of lessons must be written. Let us repeat. The authors do not write the lessons. The lessons, workbooks, and assessment tools are largely subcontracted to development houses. These are companies created by former publishing houses executives and editors and do the subcontracted work for Houghton Mifflin Harcourt, Scott Foresman, or McGraw-Hill. The major publishers cannot afford to keep the larger stable of editors and writers needed on staff, so it is easier to outsource much of the actual writing, design work, and editing. The publisher sends guidelines to the development house, and their editors and freelance writers create the lessons, workbooks, leveled books, and tests. The guidelines give the writer some freedom in how to introduce a skill, model a strategy, or give feedback. Once the lessons are written, editors at the publishing house review them. The authors of the program rarely review any of this work; the frequently noted lack of explicitness in many reading programs (Dewitz, Jones, and Leahy 2009) stems from the fact that much has to be written by many different people, with little time for review by the authors of the program.

Another important step is selecting and writing the literature. The student anthology mainly contains already published children's literature (excerpts in the upper grades). Free-lance writers under the direction of an editor write the leveled and decodable books. The publisher is striving for diverse cultural backgrounds, ethnicities, gender roles, and abilities. Here again state guidelines dictate what students should read. Sweet treats are banned from lessons in California, birthday parties might be excluded because of religious beliefs, and even the *Little Engine That Could* is suspect because he and all the other engines are boys (Thomas B. Fordham Institute 2004). In some reading programs the authors are intimately involved in the selection of the literature; in others they have no voice in the decision.

Eventually the sequence of skills and strategies must be aligned with the literature. In some programs the reading selections are organized into loosely designed themes and the skills are then fitted to the selections. In other programs the skill sequence is laid out first and the stories are matched to the selections. There is no perfect fit. One particular unit or theme may contain stories that do not revolve around a common theme, but the selections centered in another theme may combine to become an exciting unit. In some units the skills and strategies are poorly matched to the reading selection; in other units the match is elegant.

All reading programs are a result of numerous compromises. There is the fundamental compromise between teaching reading as skill development and teaching reading as a constructive process. There is the compromise between a literature-based approach and a skills approach. Ultimately there is the compromise between what the research recommends and what the educational marketplace demands. Any basal program that seeks to remain financially viable will do so because of a long series of compromises.

Are Core Reading Programs Built on Reading Research?

Core reading programs are based on scientific reading research and on market research; the market research is more vital, because it directly influences the sales of the program. Core programs do not lead, they follow the trends and adapt to them. Through market research, the publisher determines the needs and desires of the consumer. For example, small-group reading instruction has been a mainstay of the classroom at least since the mid 1990s, with the publication of *Guided Reading* (Fountas and Pinnell 1996). As this style of instruction grew in acceptance and use and was validated by research (Taylor et al. 2000), core programs began to add leveled books.

There are a number of reasons why core reading programs should not be labeled scientifically based reading research. First, while core programs provide the lessons to teach the skills and strategies validated by research, they do so in a way that is not faithful to the research (Dewitz, Jones, and Leahy 2009). Strategies are introduced with less than explicit explanation, and the amount of review and guided practice is very often much less than the original researchers intended. Second, many well-validated instructional ideas never make their way into a core program, including decoding by analogy (Gaskins et al. 1991), reciprocal teaching (Palincsar and Brown 1984), book clubs (McMahon and Raphael 1997), and transactional strategy instruction (Brown et al. 1996). Third, some very necessary ingredients for reading growth, like reading widely and deeply (Brenner and Hiebert 2010), are not present in core programs. (Core programs do not push what their publishers are not selling, so they don't trumpet independent reading.) Fourth, core reading programs have rarely been compared with one another in well-controlled studies to validate their effectiveness. When such broad studies have been tried, the researchers concluded that teacher effectiveness counted more than the program characteristics (Bond and Dykstra 1967; Piasta et al. 2009). Finally, there is much that is not known about how to teach reading, and the use of the label *research-based* conveys a certainty that does not exist.

How Should Reading Be Taught?

If a core reading program is not a research-based document that must be followed with fidelity, how should it be used? The core program is a collection of tools, and teachers must select the right tool for the job. Many of the texts and lessons in a core program are quite useful and can form the backbone of reading instruction. Often, however, the program must be supplemented. You may need to teach skills and strategies more explicitly than the program suggests. You may need to provide more small-group instruction than is outlined in the program. Your better readers will most likely need to read trade books and novels. Your struggling readers will need more supportive practice with more leveled texts than your core program can provide.

We hope this history and insight about how reading programs are created gives you the ammunition and wherewithal to break free from the five-day lesson plan repeated thirty times in a school year. Teaching reading in this way focuses on routines—teach skills, read stories, ask questions, complete workbooks, assess. This focus may cause you to forget the long-term question all teachers need to think about—what kind of readers do you want your students to become? Don't we want to create readers who love to read, use it as a tool to learn, and read critically and insightfully? Routines will not get you there. By focusing too much on skills, you and your students may miss the rewards that reading can bring. We want you to have the confidence to build and use your knowledge to create joyful experiences. This book will help you achieve this for each of your students.

Extending Your Learning

Here are two activities that can help you reflect and broaden your understanding of core reading programs. In our experience, it is helpful to complete these activities with the other teachers on your team.

1. Compare how a core reading program directs you to teach reading with another approach or framework, such as guided reading or "four blocks." Compare the daily or weekly lessons. How do these frameworks differ in organization and in their philosophy about teaching reading? Can elements of other frameworks be included in your core reading program?

2. Take the six manuals in your core reading program and write down week by week all the vocabulary or comprehension skills you will teach this year in the order they appear in the program. Are the last lessons different from the first? Will you, at the end of the year, be teaching skills your students should have mastered? Will they be working more independently at the end of the year than they were at the beginning of the year?

Further Reading

Brenner, D., and E. H. Heibert. 2010. "If I Follow the Teacher's Edition, Isn't That Enough? Analyzing Reading Volume in Six Core Reading Programs." *The Elementary School Journal* 110 (3): 347–63.

Dewitz, P., S. Leahy, J. Jones, and P. Sullivan. 2010. *The Essential Guide to Selecting and Using Core Reading Programs.* Newark, DE: International Reading Association.

Dewitz, P., J. Jones, and S. Leahy. 2009. "Comprehension Strategy Instruction in Core Reading Programs." *Reading Research Quarterly* 44 (7): 102–26.

CHAPTER 2

Think Beyond Your Core Reading Program's Five-Day Lesson Plan

A week before classes were to begin, Jonni's principal asked her to meet with the school's three first-grade teachers to help them plan their reading instruction. Ms. Graham and Mrs. Longman were new to the school and to teaching; Mrs. Allen had twenty-plus years under her belt. None were shy and all came brimming with questions and concerns. Ms. Graham asked, "How long should I spend on a reading selection?" "If the main basal selection is too easy for my best readers should I move them to a harder book?" Mrs. Longman wanted to know. Mr. Allen's question: "How many centers should I have and how often do I need to change them?" All three wondered how many times their students should read the leveled books.

The concerns of these teachers, especially the newest teachers, are predictable and consistent with what we know about how teachers use educational materials to create instruction. According to research by Gene Hall and Shirley Hord (2000), teachers go through a series of stages as they use new materials. At first they just want information about the materials—questions like "When are the leveled books read each week?" Then their concerns turn personal: "How will I manage all of this?" Eventually the focus turns to managing the materials and integrating them with old-favorite activities: "Will I be able to read my novels aloud to my class as I have always done?" As teachers become comfortable with the organization and content of the instructional material, their attention shifts to student growth: "Will these decodable books improve the reading ability of my students?" Ultimately teachers learn to innovate and use the instructional materials in ways that best help their students. Our purpose is to help all teachers make the best instructional decisions with the materials at hand.

What Research Says About How Teachers Use Reading Programs

Research over forty-five years has consistently found that teachers' knowledge, skill, and motivation play a larger role in student achievement than does the program they are using (Bond and Dykstra 1967; Piasta et al. 2009). We know that about half of the teachers use a core reading program selectively and the rest follow it faithfully. When it is followed with fidelity at least 25 percent of students do not achieve an adequate score on their state reading test (McGill-Franzen et al. 2006). Teachers regularly make decisions when they use a core reading program, and these decisions are often tailored to the demands of the texts and the needs of the students (Barr and Sadow 1989). Knowledgeable teachers avoid the skill and drill of the programs; "they are discriminating consumers who view basal readers as just one instructional tool available to them as they plan literacy lessons" (Baumann and Heubach 1996, 522).

THIS CHAPTER WILL HELP YOU:

- Begin your school year.
- Set reading goals for and with your students that stretch beyond the core program.
- Allocate time for reading instruction and restructure the routine in your core program.
- Plan a unit and a week of instruction, including whole-group, small-group, and independent activities.
- Select appropriate assessments from within and outside your core program.

The Planning Guides in Your Core Reading Program

All core reading programs have a similar structure. The programs are organized by grade level, and within each grade the programs are divided into units or themes. Except for kindergarten and first grade, each grade-level program has six themes, each lasting five to six weeks, covering an academic year. Each theme is then divided into four to six weekly (five-day) lesson plans. Instruction in core programs is standardized. The program developers expect you to follow the lessons as written and imply that if you do, your students will make progress.

The teacher's major planning task is to select among the many materials and lessons the program provides. For example, each weekly lesson plan includes many different skills lessons covering word identification, fluency, vocabulary, comprehension, grammar, and writing. In addition, there are an abundance of workbook activities. The core program provides more activities than any teacher or student can complete in a day, in part to impress buyers with the program's breadth and thoroughness. Think of all these lesson elements as features on a new car. You will be more tempted to buy a car that has a six-CD changer, heated seats, and keyless entry, even if these features have nothing to do with the quality of the car's ride or its reliability. As dedicated teachers, however, you know that you begin planning reading instruction before you examine the material.

Beginning the School Year

Beginning the school year requires equal measures of organization, discipline, patience, and inspiration. Into every kindergarten classroom enter twenty-five (give or take) little people teachers know absolutely nothing about. Have they attended a quality preschool? Do they speak English? How many of them are going to cry every day the first week? Can they follow a set of directions? Are they read to at home? Teachers in subsequent grades face similar concerns. They may be getting students new to their school whom they know little about. They may be getting the infamous holy terror from the year before. Did the previous year's teacher prepare the students for the current year?

Core reading programs give teachers few tools for starting the year. What they do provide at each grade, except in kindergarten, is a series of lessons that review what has been taught the year before. A first-grade program includes lessons covering all the letter-sound associations and high-frequency words taught in kindergarten. A second-grade program includes a quick review of phonemic awareness, phonics, high-frequency words, and a read-aloud to review comprehension strategies. These lessons are geared to the whole class and provide little help for the biggest issues at the start of the school year, which are:

1. Getting to know your students, their abilities, likes, dislikes, and temperament.
2. Teaching students the routine of your classroom and working with them until they are able to follow it.
3. Creating an exciting literate environment by stressing the books they will read and the projects they will create.

Learning about your students is critical. Some incoming students have a vast vocabulary and advanced reading skills, while others struggle with basic reading skills. Yet core programs expect much of the instruction to take place in a whole-group setting in which differentiated instruction is least likely. Teachers also need to draw a quick bead on the social and emotional skills of their students. Who will be obedient, who defiant, who responds to praise and who to attention? The success of a complex classroom routine depends on knowing your students and how to guide them. To start the year you need to be a kid watcher in every sense of the word.

Kid watching can start with formal and informal measures. Most schools give some beginning-of-the-year reading assessment to their students, and results are typically available from previous years. Nationally, schools are using the Dynamic Indicators of Basic Early Literacy Skills (DIBELS) (Good and Kaminski 2005), the Texas Primary Reading Inventory (TPRI) (Texas Education Agency 1998), or the Phonological Awareness Literacy Screening (PALS) (Invernizzi, Meier, and Juel 2003) to place students in instructional groups. Many current core reading programs recommend using these assessment tools and may also provide their own placement tests in which students read short passages and answer multiple-choice comprehension questions. Since the validity of aspects of DIBELS and the other tests has been questioned, we advocate informal measures. It is wise to construct your own assessment of kindergartners' letter and letter-sound knowledge and phonemic awareness (see Adams et al. 1998). Running records (an element of all core reading programs) are an ideal way to match students in the upper grades to leveled texts.

On the first day of school, establishing classroom management rules and classroom routines is a priority. Children thrive on structure, and learning cannot flourish in chaos. After being made aware of acceptable behavior and the necessity of following basic directions, children need to learn the procedures of reading instruction. Those procedures, especially changing activities or centers and moving from the teacher's table to a variety of independent activities, can be complex. Students need to understand what is expected of them. Following these steps is helpful:

1. Develop a few simple independent activities, so that students focus on the management routine and not the activity. Kindergartners or first graders can practice matching letters with pictures, listening to a story on tape/CD, or reading in the library corner. Older students can practice independent reading or writing.

2. Tell students why they are doing these activities and give them opportunities to practice them every day, so that they are comfortable working independently. Tell them they are learning how to behave and work independently in the classroom.

3. Provide corrective feedback and praise to keep students engaged.

4. Practice the transitions from one activity to another.

Create a management board displaying the name and a picture of each independent center, listing the names of students going to that center underneath. The management board should be placed where the students can see it since it changes every day. This board tells students what to do when you are busy teaching. Don't expect this to go smoothly at the beginning. It may take many weeks for some students to learn the routine as well as the center activities.

In our favorite classrooms reading and writing is the focus. Teachers and students share books and writing as a community of readers and writers. The hub of the room is the classroom library, a special space containing many books, arranged by genre, level, and topic. A rug and beanbag chairs on the floor and book covers on the wall create an inviting environment. Students note the books they like on a wall chart—a classroom bestsellers list. Around the room are teacher- and-student-made charts capturing the topics being studied, the strategies students are using, and the new words they are learning. Charts developed in the classroom have much more power than anything purchased at the teacher supply store. Another wall displays the students' work, the products they have created. Such print-rich classrooms promote reading comprehension (Hoffman et al. 2004).

From the first day students anticipate the books they will read, the authors they will study, and the projects they will complete. Our favorite teachers convey the excitement of reading, not the routine of skill instruction. Each day for the first week teachers introduce new authors and books. They discuss the projects students will be working on and show samples from the previous year. Students share their favorite authors and books and talk about projects they completed in a previous grade. The routine of skills instruction makes itself known without an overt introduction.

Setting Goals for Your Students

A core reading program expects you to follow a series of five-day lesson plan within a four- to six-week unit of instruction. At the end of each lesson and the unit, the program provides assessments that measure students' vocabulary, the skills they have attained, and their ability to read a passage at grade level by answering open-ended and multiple-choice comprehension questions. It is presumed but never directly stated that if students pass these end-of-lesson and end-of-unit tests they will be ready for the next grade level. We believe that the core reading programs do not set explicit goals because the publishers don't want to be held accountable, but we believe you should set goals and communicate them to your students, their parents, and the school's administrators.

Goals can be expressed quantitatively and qualitatively. A quantitative goal, for example, states that 90 percent of your third graders will pass your state assessment in reading or 100 percent of your first graders will read at level I in the Fountas and Pinnell Benchmark Assessment System (2008). These assessments define students' achievement as a level or degree of performance. Qualitative goals reflect the kinds of fiction and nonfiction books you expect your students to read, the depth and breadth of their reading, and the meaning they make from and responses they have to their reading. Figure 2.1 lists some sample quantitative

Figure 2.1.   Sample Quantitative and Qualitative Reading Goals

	Quantitative Goals	**Qualitative Goals**	
Grade Level	**Reading Assessment** (using *Qualitative Reading Inventory–5*)	**Reading Behavior** Read independently and widely from books like:	**Strategy/Thinking Goals** (from the Common Core)
K		*Pancakes for Breakfast* (dePaola) *My Five Senses* (Aliki)	Retell familiar stories with support
1	Read instructionally at a second-grade level or level I (Fountas and Pinnell)	*Little Bear* (Minarik) *Starfish* (Hurd)	Ask and answer questions Retell story details, elements
2	Read instructionally at a third-grade level or at level L (Fountas and Pinnell)	*Junie B. Jones* (Park) *From Seed to Plant* (Gibbons)	Ask and answer questions to demonstrate awareness of a story's key ideas Retell stories, fables, folktales, including central message
3	Read instructionally at a fourth-grade level or at level O (Fountas and Pinnell)	*Sarah Plain and Tall* (MacLachlan) *Moonshot: The Flight of Apollo 11* (Floca)	Ask and answer questions to demonstrate awareness of a story's key ideas Retell stories, fables, folktales, including central message
4	Read instructionally at a fifth-grade level or at level R (Fountas and Pinnell)	*Diary of a Wimpy Kid* (Kinney) *Discovering Mars* (Berger)	Use details to explain and make inferences Determine themes of and summarize stories
5	Read instructionally at a sixth-grade level or at level U (Fountas and Pinnell)	*Where the Mountain Meets the Moon* (Lin) *A History of U.S.* (Hakim)	Quote accurately from a text to explain it Use details to make inferences Determine themes Recognize character responses Summarize stories

and qualitative goals. We used *Qualitative Reading Inventory–5* (Leslie and Caldwell 2011) to determine the quantitative goals and the Common Core State Standards (www .corestandards.org) to determine the qualitative goals. Grade-level teams within each school should set their own goals, identify specific milestone books to make these goals concrete, and share this information with students and parents.

You should keep your goals constantly in mind and use them to drive your instruction. A second-grade teacher should strive for students to read and comprehend at a third-grade instructional level by the end of the year. This means starting with the short texts in the core reading program but then moving all students into the wider world of children's literature. By the middle of the year students should read independently books like *Junie B. Jones* (Park 2001), possibly *Charlotte's Web* (White 2001) and *From Seed to Plant* (Gibbons 1993). Instruction should move steadily from oral to silent reading and encourage students to read longer chunks of text without support. Independent reading must be an important and daily part of the curriculum, something that reading program manuals barely acknowledge.

Do not keep these goals a secret. Share them with your students, their parents, and your administrators. Tell your students that by the end of the year, perhaps much earlier, they will be reading exciting books like the ones listed in Figure 2.1. Tell them that a good reader is someone who reads often and enjoys it. Tell your students' parents that they can judge the progress of their children by the kinds of books they are reading and how often they read at home. Watch the excitement in a child's eyes when she reads her first chapter book.

Considering Standards—Common Core, Your State, and Your District

Our goal-setting approach is based on qualitative goals drawn from the Common Core State Standards developed by the National Governors' Association and the Council of Chief State School Officers. These standards, which have been adopted by forty-five states, itemize specific reading goals for each grade level, K–12. Your state may have adopted these standards or may be using their own.

The Common Core State Standards identify the kinds of books and texts students should read, as well as the kind of thinking these books demand. As students progress through the grades, they should read and understand increasingly complex types of fiction and nonfiction and engage in increasingly complex interpretation and analysis. They should be able to:

- Detect key ideas, make inferences, and summarize.
- Understand and use the text structure to build understanding.

- Use the writer's craft, such as word choice and figurative language, to guide their comprehension.
- Compare one aspect of text with another.
- Integrate knowledge and understanding from one text to another and combine ideas from print and visual media.

At each grade level these standards become more complex, so that eventually students are ready for college or career work.

Common Core, state, or district standards guide how you use a core reading program. First, read through the standards adopted by your school and compare them with the knowledge, skills, and strategies your program seeks to teach. Study the teacher's editions to overview the curriculum for the year. All publishers will say they have correlated their programs to whatever set of standards you will be using, but these correlations are more a marketing tool than a guide to instruction. The standards often express a depth of thinking not found in the core programs and will therefore lead to more thoughtful instruction. For example, here are two descriptions of the role of characters in a story, one from a third-grade core program, the other from the corresponding Common Core State Standards:

- *Reading program version:* Stories have characters. They are the people in the story, and their actions move the plot along.
- *Common Core standard:* Describe characters in a story (e.g., their traits, motivations, or feelings) and explain how their actions contribute to the sequence of events.

The reading program example focuses on how characters' actions advance the plot of the story; the Common Core State Standard considers plot but also character traits, feelings, and motivations, leading to deeper, more thoughtful understanding. The Common Core State Standards also make explicit the kinds of books students should be reading, recommending texts of greater length and complexity than those in a core reading program. The short texts in a core reader are useful for modeling and explaining a strategy or a concept, but books are necessary for developing reading ability.

Allocating Time for Reading Instruction

Time is precious in school and many people are fighting for it. The physical education teacher wants more of it so students stay slim and healthy. The drug awareness teacher needs an hour a week to make sure your students stay clean. The counselor wants a piece of it so she can help your students develop good character. Kids should really eat lunch, play at recess, and go to the bathroom. Some of the demands for time are beyond your control, but some are not.

We hope you work in a school where the principal has allocated an uninterrupted block of time for reading/language arts instruction. *Uninterrupted* means time not split in half by lunch, recess, or occasional assemblies. It means students do not leave for art, music, or PE. *Uninterrupted* also means not using the public address system during instructional periods to summon children to the office or announce the winner of last night's PTA door prize. It means the school secretary does not ring your classroom phone. If you don't work in a school like this, encourage your principal to change his or her ways. According to research findings, effective reading/language arts instruction requires a minimum of 100 to 130 minutes per day (Allington and Cunningham 2002). We believe schools should schedule the same amount of time for reading in the primary and upper grades; there is much to learn and read at all levels.

Divide your uninterrupted block of time among whole-group and small-group instruction and independent learning activities. Figure 2.2 suggests a way of allocating instructional time with a heterogeneous class composed of advanced readers, average readers, and readers who struggle.

Effective teachers spend about sixty minutes total in small-group instruction; ineffective teachers, about half that amount (Taylor et al. 2000). This time is essential so teachers can differentiate instruction. They also provide ample amounts of time for independent work, because students in the most effective classrooms read real books and articles and write for real audiences and real purposes (Pressley et al. 2002). Some of the independent reading and writing time will be used for whole-class writing lessons; in some cases, very effective teachers find time to see the weakest students again. Just five minutes of additional instructional time for struggling readers adds up to fifteen additional hours of instruction during

Figure 2.2.   Allocating Instructional Time

	Whole-Group Instruction	Small-Group Instruction	Independent Reading and Writing
Above-Level Readers	30 min/day	15–20 min/day	75–80 min/day
On-Level Readers	30 min/day	20–25 min/day	70–75 min/day
Below-Level Readers	30 min/day	25–30 min/day	65–70 min/day

the year, time that can make a significant difference for many students (Connor, Morrison, Fishman et al. 2007). Finally, effective teachers spend considerably less small-group time with the strongest readers, not out of neglect but knowing that these students thrive when they are working alone or with a partner on important projects (Connor et al. 2009).

Planning a Unit of Instruction with Your Core Program

Planning reading instruction requires understanding your students, formulating specific goals, and deciding what materials will help you reach those goals. The core reading program provides many of the texts, lessons, and materials needed for effective reading instruction, however, it's not your complete reading program. You will need to reach beyond the program to create effective reading instruction that will promote a stimulating reading experience.

Core reading programs are organized into themes, four to six weekly lessons within each theme. The theme overview outlines the reading skills and strategies that will be taught in the unit, the selections and books the students will read, a suggested project to motivate students and integrate what they will be learning, and the tools for assessing students progress along the way and at the end of the unit. The unit teacher's manual has sections with headings like Theme Resources (books, selections, workbooks), Theme Project, Theme at a Glance (list of skills and strategies), and Monitor Progress (assessment tools). The units or themes have titles like Relationships, Follow Me, and New Frontiers. These titles imply that a common set of ideas will be developed as the students read the selections. This is rarely the case, because the reading selections do not build knowledge systematically from one selection to another (Walsh 2003; Dewitz et al. 2010). Often you must add reading selections, read-alouds, and other activities so that the instructional units have more substance and build students' knowledge. There are also times when you might not read a selection from a core program because it is unrelated to the other selections, substituting another book or article instead.

Theme Project

Start by building substantive units around the *theme projects* suggested by the core program or create your own. A theme project is a cumulative activity that draws on all the skills, knowledge, and vocabulary learned over four to six weeks. Since much of reading instruction takes place when students are working in small groups, with a partner, or individually, the theme project gives all students a common purpose. It interrupts the teach-practice-assess routine of reading instruction. These projects are often neglected and shouldn't be. They build community as all children, regardless of ability, share and contribute.

Projects and activities provide more tangible motivation than the "learn these skills and you will be a better reader" approach. Children's strategy and skills grow when they read and write for a purpose (Guthrie et al. 2000). Many of the projects in teacher's manuals are good ideas, but you can often add to them or create your own more substantial project. For example, one core program has students create a self-portrait collage. The students draw an outline of themselves and fill it with pictures cut from magazines that illustrate their likes, dislikes, favorite activities, friends, and family. While this is an engaging idea, it is only one lesson and does little to integrate the readings within or outside the core program. The Relationships unit of another program has the students interview a parent, grandparent, or teacher and present the findings to the class. In class work surrounding this project students discuss the characteristics of important relationships as depicted in the selections from the core program. Then they learn to question, organize, think, write, and present their interview.

Here are our guidelines for effective theme projects:

- Create a project that engages the students and leads to a tangible product: a piece of writing, an art piece, a PowerPoint presentation, a play, or a video.

- Design a project that will be appropriate for all students.

- Create a model of the finished project so that students understand the goal.

- Require students to incorporate into the final product what they have learned from reading within and outside the core program (books, magazines, the Internet).

- List and describe the steps the students must take to complete the project.

- Provide time for students to work on their project. This is why we believe in larger chunks of time spent working independently.

- If the project requires some cooperative work, show students how to work together. Gauge the abilities of your students and jigsaw components of the project so that all students are engaged and appropriately challenged.

Planning Skills and Strategies

The next step in planning is to study the *theme planner* or *unit planner* provided at the beginning of the appropriate volume of the teacher's edition. Figure 2.3 is our version of a core reading program's planner for a first-grade unit taught early in the school year. It lays out the instructional objective for the discovery theme and lists the skills, strategies, and

Figure 2.3.   Theme Planner 1: A Unit of Discovery

	Lesson 1	Lesson 2
Oral Language		
• **Phonological awareness**	Segment phonemes: Initial sounds	Segment phonemes: Initial sounds
• **Question of the Day**	Why is exploring so much fun?	How do we make new friends?
• **Oral vocabulary**	Read-aloud	Read-aloud
Word Work		
• **Phonics skills**	Short /a/ *s* ✓	Short /a/ *a* ✓
• **Spelling**	Consonants: *t, m, r, p, s*	Consonants: *v, z, h, l, b, g*
Vocabulary		
• **High-frequency words**	*in, too , now*	*let's, help, no*
• **Content vocabulary**	*valley, mountain, sense, escape, unexpected, sweltering*	*sandwich, practice, dinner, cafeteria, utensils, permission*
Reading		
• **Main selection**	*Carlo and Isabelle's Big Adventure* (narrative)	*Challah and Bagel Go to School* (narrative)
• **Comprehension**	Details ✓	Characters ✓
	Make predictions ✽	Summarizing ✽
• **Fluency**	Sight word review	Phrase reading
Language Arts		
• **Grammar**	Sentences	Naming part of sentences: Nouns
• **Writing**	Writing labels	Writing declarative sentences

✓ Tested Skills   ✽ Focus Strategy

Grade 1

Lesson 3	Lesson 4	Lesson 5
Oral Language		
Isolate phonemes	Rhyme recognition	Segment phonemes: Final consonants
How do plants help us survive?	How does the moon influence our life?	How do we solve problems?
Read-aloud	Read-aloud	Read-aloud
Word Work		
Short /i/ *I* ✓	Phonograms: *ap, at, ag, an* ✓	Phonograms: *it, ip, im, id* ✓
Inflection: *s*	Inflection: *ed, ing*	Contractions: *n't*
Vocabulary		
hold, home, get, late	*oh, yes, run, play*	*now, make, some, thank*
plant, seed, fertilizer, stem, roots, leaves	*star, sun, mood, tides, meteor*	*Africa, plains, roaming, sensed, memorize, solutions*
Reading		
A Plant Grows (information)	*A Starry Night* (information)	*The Ant and the Zebra*
Expository text ✓	Graphic features ✓	Character ✓
Questions ✳	Evaluate ✳	Visualize ✳
Partner reading	Sight word review	Echo reading
Language Arts		
Telling parts of sentences: Verbs	Writing questions	Punctuation: Capitals and periods
Description: Group writing	Description: Group writing	Creating a class story

selections you are to teach in each individual lesson. (Teacher's manuals may use either the term *week* or *lesson*: one lesson equals one week.) Some themes require four weeks of instruction, others, five or six; it depends on the publisher and the grade level.

The far left-hand column of Figure 2.3 lists the domains to be covered in each lesson—*oral language*, *word work*, *vocabulary*, *reading*, and *language arts*. The lessons are listed left to right in columns next to the domains that identify the focus for each week. The check mark following some of these skills indicates that the skill will be tested at the end of the lesson or the unit. Important skills are designated with an asterisk but are not assessed.

Read through the sample theme planner and note the skills, strategies, and selections the core program recommends. What do you notice about the number of skills and strategies and the volume of reading? Continue your planning by examining each domain, lesson by lesson. Focus on these questions: *Are these the right skills for my students? Will I be teaching too many skills each week? Is the vocabulary sufficient? Have my students already mastered some of these skills?* We will return to these questions when we examine an individual lesson.

ORAL LANGUAGE.   In this domain the core program each week suggests phonemic awareness activities, a question of the day to stimulate discussion, and a read-aloud. The phonemic awareness activity moves from the initial sound of phonemes the first week to isolating phonemes the third week and then on to rhyme recognition. The research on phonemic awareness reveals this is not a developmental sequence, and you might want to change the focus of the lessons. Also consider the skill of your students. If they are phonemically aware, these lessons might not be necessary. Or the read-aloud and the question of the day might be redundant. With some adaptation you can embed good questions within your read-aloud. Read-alouds are essential for young students, English language learners, and any students who come from an impoverished literacy background. (We discuss the read-aloud in more depth in the next chapter.)

WORD WORK AND VOCABULARY.   The word work section—phonics and spelling—presents a reasonable sequence of phonic patterns to be taught early in first grade. However it was designed for hypothetical learners, not the students in your classroom. Some will need these skills, others will have already mastered them. You might find the early emphasis on individual letter sounds and the later emphasis on phonograms to be the wrong order. You could change this sequence and teach different skills in small groups based on the needs of your students. (We expand on these suggestions in Chapter 4.) The vocabulary section merely lists the words you need to teach; we will return to that area when we consider planning lessons.

READING.   This domain encompasses selections the students will read, comprehension skills and strategies they will learn, and fluency activities. The selections, read each week, include those from the pupils' edition and in the leveled and decodable books. These few selections are not enough reading for students to become strong fluent readers; they need to be supplemented (Brenner and Hiebert 2010). We recommend at least four or five leveled books a week for the youngest students. This means that for each weekly lesson you will need to look for additional texts for students to read. Stronger and older readers can read fewer but longer books.

This domain also lists four comprehension skills (details, characters, expository text structure, graphic features) and five comprehension strategies (predicting, summarizing, questioning, evaluating, and visualizing) to be taught in five weeks of instruction. These are too many skills for most students to learn and use in any meaningful way (Dewitz, Jones, and Leahy 2009), let alone to expect from first graders. Your first task is to limit what you plan to teach. One or two skills and one or two strategies per unit are sufficient. In this particular unit three of the selections are narrative, so teaching about and discussing characters make sense. The other two selections are informational text, so a focus on graphic features is appropriate. Predicting, self-questioning, making inferences, summarizing, and monitoring comprehension are all critical strategies (Brown and Dewitz in press). We would pick predicting and questioning and make them the focus for the whole unit. The rest of the skills and strategies can wait until next year, or they can be introduced during small-group instruction to those students who are ready. The fluency activities jump from one activity to another with no consistent plan for the unit. Some of these activities, like sight word review and partner reading, will take place every day.

Using the Theme Resources

The theme resources section lists the materials and resources included in the program—big books for read-alouds, teacher's manuals and student anthologies, decodable books, leveled readers, consumable workbooks, and so on. Decide what you will use, what you will omit, and what needs to be added. We offer the following guidelines:

- Use the reading selections in the student anthology to introduce and model concepts, skills, and strategies.

- Use the leveled books and decodable books for guided reading. However, for your better readers, be prepared to move beyond these selections into nonfiction trade books, chapter books, and novels. For your weaker readers you will need more leveled texts—three or four per week.

- Start searching your school library for more books to read aloud.

- Drastically limit your use of workbooks and worksheets. These do not promote the depth of thinking your students require (Leinhardt, Zigmond, and Cooley 1981). Additional reading and engaging writing projects provide better practice. (We provide some workbook guidelines in Chapter 4.)

Figure 2.4, My Theme Planning Guide, shows you some possible modifications to a first-grade theme, new adventures. The left-hand column lists the major elements in the theme. The middle column lists the texts, materials, and ideas suggested in the teacher's edition. The right column lists our suggested modifications and additions. We discuss our thinking below. You can do the same kind of planning using the blank version of form at the end of the chapter (Figure 2.10).

We changed the theme in a number of ways. First, we narrowed the scope so instead of New Adventures the students are studying Animals In and Out of the Zoo. For the theme project the students create their own little animal books, which expand on the core program's suggestion. Many books are provided for read-alouds and all tie to the theme of the unit. We reduced the number of skills to be taught and added many leveled books for the students to read. Better readers move into trade books.

Planning a Week of Instruction with Your Core Program
• •

Every core program provides a suggested five-day lesson plan for introducing and practicing skills and strategies, reading texts, and assessing students. The lesson plan directs your instruction and ultimately guides how you think about reading instruction, emphasizing the piecemeal skills approach over knowledge acquisition and student engagement. The My Weekly Lesson Planning Guide template at the end of the chapter (Figure 2.11) will help you plan your weekly instruction.

Figure 2.5 is our simulation of a five-day lesson plan for the third week of the first unit in a second-grade core reading program. Note the skill, strategies, and reading selections identified. You may find undue repetition, poor sequencing of activities, or an insufficient amount of text for students to read. Like the sample theme planner in Figure 2.3, the sample lesson planner covers the same five domains: oral language, word work, vocabulary, reading (comprehension and fluency), and language arts. The plan emphasizes whole-class lessons, which is true for five-day plans in all core reading programs published before 2008. Core reading programs published after 2008 include an additional five-day plan for small-group

Figure 2.4. My Theme Planning Guide

Grade Level: _First_		Unit/Theme: _New Adventures_
	What the Core Program Provides	**Your Modifications and Additions**
Theme Focus	New Adventures	Wild Animals In and Out of the Zoo
Theme Project	Children discuss animals in cooperative groups. They list names of animals. Each student makes a diagram, drawing/writing a surprising fact about their favorite animal.	Students build their own zoo book, researching, drawing, and writing about a particular animal. Each book will focus on characteristics of the animal. The books will be "published" and shared with the class.
Word Work and Vocabulary	Consonants—*t, m, r, s*, etc. Short *a, i*, and phonograms High-frequency words Content vocabulary	On- and below-level students follow the core scope and sequence Above-level students work on long vowel patterns—cvc*e*, cvv*e*
Comprehension Skills/Strategies	Details Predicting Characters Visualizing Expository text Graphic features Questioning Evaluating	Predicting Questioning Narrative text—characters Expository text—details
Read-Aloud Texts for Teacher Modeling	Student anthology selections *Big Book of Animals* Read-alouds in the teacher's manual	Student anthology selections **Read-alouds:** *A True Book—Mammals* (nonfiction) *Bear Snores On* (fiction) *Bats* (nonfiction) *Stelluna* (fiction) *The Crocodile: Ruler of the River* (nonfiction) *Bill and Pete* (fiction)
Leveled Books for Guided Reading **Trade Books**	Main anthology selections (one per lesson/student) Decodable books (one per lesson/student)	Additional leveled readers from Reading A–Z and from Ready Readers for short *a* patterns Short chapter book—*Frog and Toad*—for above level students

Figure 2.5.   Suggested Lesson Plan Unit 1, Week 3

	Day 1	Day 2
Oral Language		
• **Phonological awareness** • **Question of the Day** • **Oral vocabulary**	Segment: Onsets and rimes How do you think lizards and dinosaurs are alike? Read-aloud: Lizard, turtle, scales, cold-blooded	Phoneme categorization What can we learn at the zoo? Review vocabulary from read-aloud, 32N
Word Work		

• **Phonics skills**
 	
• **Spelling**
	✓ Phonics: Make words with /a/ *a*
	   Practice book A, O, B: 1
	✓ Spelling: Pretest short *a*
		✓ Phonics: Make words with /a/
		   a 13G
		✓ Spelling: Word sort, *a, i*

Vocabulary		
• **Content vocabulary** • **Vocabulary strategy**	✓ *explore, discover, excited, terrified,* *sudden, whisper* ✓ Use the dictionary: Practice book A, O, B	Review words in context
Reading		
• **Selections** • **Comprehension** • **Fluency**	Decodable: *Lizards Can Go* Strategy: Story Structure ✓ Skill details Echo reading, 31G	Anthology: "Second Grade Visits the Zoo" Strategy: Story Structure, 39C ✓ Skill details, 39D Word fluency, 31G
Language Arts		
• **Grammar** • **Writing**	Daily language activity ✓ Sentences: Statements Personal narrative: Group write	Daily language activity ✓ Sentences: Questions Personal narrative: Brainstorm

✓ Tested Skill

Essential Skills: Short vowels, dictionary usage, details, story structure

Day 3	Day 4	Day 5
Oral Language		
Segment: Onsets and rimes What does Juan like to do?	Phoneme segmentation Where should Juan look to learn more about lizards?	Phoneme categorization What strategy helped you understand the story this week?
Word Work		
✓ Phonics: Make words with /a/ *a* 13H ✓ Spelling: Word sort, *a, i*	✓ Phonics: Make words with /a/ *a* 15B ✓ Spelling: Spelling book, 4	✓ Phonics: Weekly assessment ✓ Spelling: Assessment
Vocabulary		
Review words in context Use the dictionary, 27B	Review words in context Use the dictionary, 33H	Assess content vocabulary
Reading		
Anthology: "Second Grade Visits the Zoo" ✓ Review skill characters and setting, 39D Partner reading, 31I	Leveled Readers: See small-group lessons ✓ Skill details, 39J Practice book A, O, B, 8 Echo reading, 33C	Self-Selected Reading ✓ Skill details, assessment
Language Arts		
Daily language activity ✓ Sentences: Capitalization Personal narrative: Topic sentences	Daily language activity ✓ Sentences: Punctuation Personal narrative: Revising	Daily language activity ✓ Sentences: Punctuation Personal narrative: Share

instruction. Core programs rarely tell you how much time to spend on whole-group and small-group instruction; their goal is to present a large number of lessons and have you decide which students need which skills. Doing everything suggested in a lesson would require more than sixty minutes of whole-group instruction and thus rob time from the more important small-group instruction and individual reading and writing.

Whole-Group Instruction

We recommend thirty to forty-five minutes of whole-group instruction a day, to include two activities (and adding, in kindergarten and first grade, a brief drill on phonics and phonemic awareness):

- Conduct a read-aloud each day focusing on vocabulary, prior knowledge, and comprehension. Read two or three books per week on the same topic, alternating a fiction and nonfiction selection (Santoro et al. 2008).

- Twice a week teach or review important comprehension skills and strategies.

- Twice a week teach and review the important vocabulary from the students' anthology and their leveled readers. Introduce or review a word-learning strategy like using the dictionary or using context clues to infer word meanings.

Small-Group Instruction

We recommend sixty minutes of small-group instruction (more for struggling readers, less for advanced students) during which you differentiate instruction and modify the core guidelines:

- *Below-level readers.* With struggling readers, focus on phonics or decoding, ignoring the skills suggested by the core program and focusing instead on the skills they need. During guided reading of a decodable book help students apply new decoding strategies and employ the comprehension strategies introduced in whole-group instruction. In their remaining lessons have them work with additional leveled readers.

- *On-level readers.* Have these students do some decoding work, but at a higher level and for less time than the struggling readers. Phonics can be incorporated into vocabulary review by showing the students how to break words down into syllables, prefixes, and suffixes. During guided reading focus on fluency and comprehension. Teacher-assisted fluency practice helps students refine their skills. Work on comprehension by helping students apply strategies to build their understanding. While the core lesson stresses one skill—details—and one strategy—story structure—we suggest helping students use a suite of strategies—predicting, questioning, summarizing, inferring—and teaching story structure in your postreading discussions. The one-skill-or-strategy-at-a-time approach has been shown to be less successful in improving comprehension compared with learning to use a suite of strategies (Reutzel, Smith, and Fawson 2005).

- *Above-level readers.* Have these students work on comprehension and vocabulary during their small-group instruction. They should also be reading fiction and nonfiction trade books outside the core program, often independently, and discussing and evaluating what they have read.

You may have noticed we did not discuss reading the main core selection from the pupils' edition. This selection presents a problem; it is too challenging for some students and too easy for others. In the primary grades we suggest that you begin reading the selection aloud and include some echo reading. Students can then finish the selection independently. In the intermediate grades, introduce the selection to all students. Those who can should read the selection independently; others can read it as part of a guided reading session with you.

Independent Work

Students who can should be reading extensively from a variety of genres and be held accountable by keeping a reading journal, sharing their favorite books, and participating in book clubs or literature circles. Students who need a little help can prepare for a guided reading lesson by generating questions, searching for new vocabulary words, and summarizing what they have read. Students who need extra practice can play decoding games or engage in timed partner reading to build fluency.

Figure 2.6 shows our approach to weekly lesson planning. We list the texts, knowledge, vocabulary, and skills on which we will focus during whole-group, small-group, and independent sessions. We don't separate it into days for two reasons. One, instruction rarely falls into five equal pieces of work. Two, we believe if we plan the week carefully we will know how to break up the work up over the five days. Figures 2.7 and 2.8 detail how we sequence the activities over five days.

Figure 2.7 presents our day-by-day plan for whole-group instruction. The activities for whole-group instruction (other than the daily drill in kindergarten and first grade) vary from day to day. We also conduct a read-aloud every day because it is important to developing vocabulary and comprehension. On some days we read a fiction book, on others a nonfiction book. (We talk more about read-alouds in the next chapter.) Vocabulary instruction is stressed two days a week; on the alternate days we introduce or practice comprehension strategies.

The focus of small-group instruction and independent work depends on the skill of the reader (Connor et al. 2004). Figure 2.8 reflects that emphasis. The above-level readers need to work on vocabulary and comprehension, while the on-level students still might need a dose of phonics, regular work on fluency, and work on comprehension and vocabulary. The below-level students need continued work on phonemic awareness, phonics, and comprehension. We are not saying that fluency and vocabulary are unimportant, but these struggling readers must first become competent in word identification (Juel and Minden-Cupp 2000).

Figure 2.6. My Weekly Lesson Planning Guide

Week of   October 1 to 5, 2013

Standards and Objective: Develop concepts of narrative structure and the characteristics of fantasy; build fluency

Lesson Focus: Animals in the Zoo
Whole-Group Instruction

Read-Alouds	Vocabulary	Comprehension	Unit Theme/Project
Giant Pandas (G. Gibbons) *Animal Strike at the Zoo* (K. Wilson)	zoo captivity breed cub China attraction bamboo caretaker	Expository text structure Narrative text structure	Each student will identify an animal typically found in a zoo and research how the animal lives in the wild. Each child will read two or three books, take notes, and develop a poster about their animal. They will then present the poster to the class.

Small-Group Instruction/Independent Work				
	Texts	Knowledge Development/ Vocabulary	Skill/Strategies Phonics Comprehension	Independent Work
Above-Level Readers	Anthology: "Second Grade Visits the Zoo" Novel: *The Secret Zoo* (Chick) Students continue to read and discuss fantasy novel; goal is to guide the students to lead their own discussions	Continue to define and explore the genre of fantasy Continue to build knowledge of zoos and the animals in them Develop a concept map	Self-questioning Narrative structure, novels Dictionary usage	• Work on animal poster • Read novel and develop discussion questions • Add words and definitions to personal dictionary • Independent writing about the novel or the animal project
On-Level Readers	Anthology: "Second Grade Visits the Zoo" Leveled Reader: *The Anteater in the Zoo* Picture Book: *New at the Zoo*	Vocabulary from the core reader, plus new words from the picture book Continue to build knowledge of zoos and the animals in them Develop a concept map	Review decoding strategies—long vowels Explore story structure Develop fluency	• Work on animal poster • Add words and definitions to personal dictionary • Read in pairs to develop fluency • Create story map for picture book
Below-Level Readers	Anthology: "Second Grade Visits the Zoo" (read-aloud) Leveled readers: *Tigers and Lions* *My Insect Zoo* Decodable book: *Pigs and Wigs*	Continue to build knowledge of zoos and the animals in them Develop a concept map Work on vocabulary selected from leveled readers Review basic sight words as needed	Work on decoding skills—short vowel words Develop fluency Explore story structure	• Work on animal poster • Add words and definitions to personal dictionary • Paired repeated readings to develop fluency • Word sorts and decoding games

Figure 2.7. Day-by-Day Whole-Group Weekly Lesson Plan

Whole-Group Instruction					
	Day 1	**Day 2**	**Day 3**	**Day 4**	**Day 5**
Daily Drill (Kindergarten and First Grade)	Sight words Phonemic awareness	Sight words Phonemic awareness	Sight words Phonemic awareness	Sight words Phonemic awareness	Sight words Phonemic awareness
Oral Language	Read-aloud 1, vocabulary	Read-aloud 1, comprehension	Read-aloud 2, vocabulary	Read-aloud 2, comprehension	Read-aloud review
Vocabulary	Content vocabulary		Word-learning strategy: dictionary		
Comprehension		Introduce new strategy: story structure		Review new strategy	

Planning Assessments

In the front of each core reading unit teacher's manual there is an inventory of the assessments available to check students' progress and diagnose problems. Programs provide weekly assessments that measure students' phonics skills, vocabulary knowledge, and use of comprehension strategies. They also provide periodic fluency assessments (typically one-minute reads); running records that assess the development of word recognition and comprehension; and end-of-unit, midyear, and end-of-year tests. Figure 2.9 lists the assessment tools typically available in a core program. You are faced with several key questions. What do you want to know about your students' progress? Which assessment tools will you use? How often will you assess?

Some of these assessments will overlap with the benchmark or interim assessment districts create or purchase to predict students' success on their state's high-stakes test. Administrators, who are not in the classroom day after day, prefer more formal approaches to assessment; teachers believe they get most of their data through class work and informal

Figure 2.8. Differentiated Small-Group Instruction and Independent Work

Small-Group Instruction					
	Day 1	**Day 2**	**Day 3**	**Day 4**	**Day 5**
Above-Level Readers	Comprehension Vocabulary	Comprehension Vocabulary	Comprehension Vocabulary	Comprehension Vocabulary	Comprehension Vocabulary
On-Level Readers	Phonics Fluency Vocabulary Comprehension	Fluency Vocabulary Comprehension	Phonics Fluency Vocabulary Comprehension	Fluency Vocabulary Comprehension	Fluency Vocabulary Comprehension
Below-Level Readers	Phonemic awareness Phonics Comprehension	Phonemic awareness Phonics Comprehension	Phonemic awareness Phonics Comprehension	Phonemic awareness Phonics Comprehension	Phonemic awareness Phonics Comprehension
Independent Activities					
All Students	Independent reading and responding with accountability, book clubs, and literature circles Writing in response to reading, journal writing				
On-Level Students	Independent reading and responding with accountability, book clubs, and literature circles Fluency practice activities Word-study activities				
Below-Level Students	Independent reading and responding with accountability, books clubs, and literature circles Fluency practice activities Word-study activities				

observations (Paris and Hoffman 2004). Core reading programs do not require that you administer any of these specific assessments; rather, they make the tools available and let you and district administrators decide. Some schools require a minimum number of grades per marking period, and end-of-week assessments fit the bill. But stopping instruction every week to devote a class period to assessment is not necessary. You can make these evaluations by taking notes while students read, answer questions, and write. We offer the following guidelines for selecting assessments:

Figure 2.9. Assessment Tools in Core Programs

Assessment Tools	Purpose and Format
Weekly Assessments	Assess skills of the week, vocabulary, grammar, and usage Use multiple-choice and constructed-response formats
Fluency Assessments	One-minute reads, often in connection with retelling or a few comprehension questions
Running Records	Graded passages for assessing word recognition, self-corrections, fluency, and retelling
End-of-Unit Assessments	Assess comprehension of what has been taught in the unit or theme Focus on specific skills, phonics, vocabulary and grammar, and writing, using multiple-choice and constructed-response formats
Benchmark or Midyear and End-of-Year Assessments	Assess the reading comprehension skills, vocabulary, and word-learning strategies taught during the period

- Assess as infrequently as possible. You do not want to consume instructional time with testing. You can't fatten a pig by weighing it.

- Employ assessments that help you make instructional decisions. Anticipate how the results of an assessment will help you make instructional decisions.

- Students who are struggling to read should be assessed more often and more diagnostically. A periodic fluency or decoding assessment will help you determine whether students are improving in these skills.

- Trust your informal observations from students' oral reading performance, classroom discussions, and written work. Use the core or district assessments to support these observations every six to nine weeks.

- Meet with your grade-level colleagues to discuss student progress and the results of the assessments. Through discussion you will understand the data, revise your goals, and gain insights about your instruction.

Extending Your Learning

We hope you are now able and eager to plan with your core reading program in a new way. Here are a few activities that can help you understand the structure of a core program and plan effectively:

1. Review one unit or theme, playing close attention to the content of the anthology selections and the leveled books. What oral read-aloud would you add to give the unit more substance? What chapter books, novels, or nonfiction trade books would you use for the stronger readers in your room?

2. Look at next week's lesson plan. Which skills will you need to teach and which skills can you avoid? Which skills, if any, will be taught to the whole group, and which can be taught in small groups?

3. Locate a copy of the Common Core State Standards (www.corestandards.org) or your district/state standards. With your grade-level colleagues compare these standards with the core reading program. Which of the standards are covered in your program and which are not? Which of the standards demand more depth than the comparable skills in the core program do?

Figure 2.10.   My Theme Planning Guide

Grade Level: _____	Unit/Theme _____	
	What the Core Program Provides	**Your Modifications and Additions**
Theme Focus		
Theme Project		
Word Work and Vocabulary		
Comprehension Skills/Strategies		
Read-Alouds for Teacher Modeling **Leveled Books for Guided Reading** **Trade Books**		

Figure 2.11. My Weekly Lesson Planning Guide

Week of _____

Standards and Objectives: _____

Whole-Group Instruction			
Read-Alouds	**Vocabulary**	**Comprehension**	**Unit Theme/Project**

Small-Group Instruction/Independent Work				
	Texts	**Knowledge Development/ Vocabulary**	**Skill/Strategies Phonics Comprehension**	**Independent Work**
Above-Level Readers				
On-Level Readers				
Below-Level Readers				

What Does the Research Say About How Children Acquire Independent Word Reading Skills?

As many of us know from our teaching, learning to read is not automatic. Unlike learning to walk, most children need the help of a knowledgeable adult to learn to read. Yet we sometimes make the assumption—which is not true—that teachers must teach every step of the reading process, every possible skill. Research indicates we don't have to be responsible for all these pieces. Rather, reading becomes a self-teaching system (Share 1995); as children read, they learn many of the skills and words on their own and build the knowledge essential for strong comprehension. Our job is to teach until children can continue successfully on their own.

How Do Children Learn to Read?

Presley is bit past her second birthday and beginning to learn to read. She sits in her big chair, wrapped in a blanket, and turns the pages of *Brown Bear, Brown Bear* (Martin and Carle 2010). On each page she names the animal and makes the sound of that animal—"moo, moo," "quack, quack." By watching and looking she has formulated an idea how print translates into meaning. As Jeanne Chall (1983) has written, Presley has a hypothesis—the idea that the pictures will tell her what to say. Later, when she begins to focus on the print, she must develop a new hypothesis about how print translates into meaning.

Fast-forward two years. Presley is now in the first stage of reading. She looks at the word *McDonald's* on the large sign and is able to recognize and remember that word because of the golden arches behind it and the drive-through window on the building underneath. Most four-year-olds can read the McDonald's sign in context, but few can read *McDonald's* when it is printed on a flashcard (Ehri 1996). At this earliest stage of reading environmental print a child is reading the context, not yet the print.

With development and experience Presley changes her thinking and creates a new idea, a new hypothesis. If a word contains a specific squiggle, visual design, or letter pattern, it is pronounced in a certain way. So the word with the squiggle letter is _stop_ and the word with two little round circles, *oo*, is _look_. This stage of development is called *visual cue reading*, a *prealphabetic* stage (Ehri 1996). This system of identifying words ignores the letter-sound correspondence that forms the basis of English. Presley remembers each individual word by some distinctive visual feature. The system works for a while until she encounters other words with squiggles, like *sleep*, *po_st_*, and *pot_s_*. Attending to just one visual cue will not help her remember many different words. So Presley must develop a better system for remembering the words and formulate a new hypothesis.

Eventually Presley begins to realize that individual letters stand for sounds. This is called the *partial alphabetic* phase of reading, since the reader attends to a few salient letters in each word, often just the initial or final letter (Ehri 2005). This is a big conceptual leap: Presley has discovered the alphabetic principle of language. A few children develop this insight on their own by inferring from the words *truck*, *tree*, and *tell*, for example, that the letter *t* make the /t/ sound. The initial clue to this insight is learning letter names, because the sound made by the letter is often in its name (Share 2004). Most children, however, will require instruction to learn the alphabetic principle. Eventually Presley learns to attend to all the letter-sound combinations in a word—the *full alphabetic* stage—and decodes most single-syllable words using phonics patterns. In the final, *consolidated alphabetic* phase, the reader moves beyond letter-sound patterns and learns and uses sublexical units of the language—prefixes, suffixes, roots, and other syllables to identify words like *exploratory* and *abnormal* (Ehri 2005).

Why Is Phonemic Awareness Critical to Learning to Read?

As any kindergarten teacher knows, discovering the alphabetic principle that letters and letter patterns stand for sounds is the critical insight necessary for learning to read. Understanding the alphabetic principle is based on two other insights—letter knowledge and phonemic awareness. Children cannot connect letters to sounds unless and until they can discriminate one letter from another (Adams 1990). This is a relatively easy task for most children and is often the product of living in a home rich with books, being read to, and even watching *Sesame Street*.

Phonemic awareness is the understanding that words consist of sounds—more specifically *phonemes*, the smallest unit of speech—and that these phonemes can be isolated, manipulated, and attached to letters (Stahl and Murray 1998). When children are learning to speak, they can easily change one phoneme for another to produce a new word (*pig* vs. *big*, for example), but they do not have to think about the process. They are not consciously aware of the phonemes. Learning to read demands a conscious awareness of phonemes, which do not have a concrete existence. Think of listening to speakers of languages you do not speak. Most of us think these people speak fast, because we can't detect the word boundaries amid the swift flow of sounds. Carried one step further, we cannot detect the individual sounds within the words. But when we can segment the phonemes, we have phonemic awareness.

Children learning to read must construct the phonemes from the speech stream, which isn't easy. The initial sound in the word *bell* is not /buh/, nor is it /bee/. The sound of the letter *b* cannot be pronounced in isolation; its sound is bound up with the vowel that follows. Yet readers must be able to hear these sounds and match them to individual letter patterns. Failing to develop phonemic awareness, children will not benefit from learning letter-sound associations or from phonics instruction (Bradley and Bryant 1983). When teachers claim that a child cannot learn phonics or has not benefited from traditional phonics instruction, the most likely culprit is the lack of phonemic awareness.

Why Is Direct Instruction in Phonics Essential for Most Students?

Phonics instruction is essential for most readers, and even for those who learn easily, a dose of phonics has no detrimental effect on learning to read (Snow and Juel 2005). Phonics instruction helps children discover the alphabetic principle and causes them to look closely at the letter-sound patterns of words. There is considerable evidence that explicit, systematic instruction in phonics contributes to students' growth in reading (Adams 1990; Oakhill and Beard 1999; National Reading Panel 2000; Tunmer and Nicholson 2011). Phonics instruction includes learning the letter-sound patterns of the language, learning to use that knowledge in a strategic way to unlock the pronunciation of new words, and learning to monitor the process so that the reader can self-correct errors and try new strategies.

Direct explicit instruction in phonics is very useful. For a small portion of the day young readers can study and learn the letter-sound patterns without being distracted by the problems of reading connected text or focusing on the meaning (Pressley 2006; Shankweiler and Crain 2004). Phonics instruction also ensures that "beginning readers see the importance of focusing on word-level cues as the most useful sources of information in identifying words and to overcome any tendency they may have to rely primarily on the sentence context cues" (Tunmer and Nicholson 2011, 417).

Will Instruction and Drill on Phonics Patterns Lead to Accurate and Fluent Word Recognition?

Although the research on phonics instruction is very positive, phonics has its limits. We cannot teach all the phonics patterns in the language. There are "simply too many letter-sound relationships for children to acquire by direct instruction, probably several hundred" (Gough and Hillinger 1980, cited in Tunmer and Nicholson 2011). Consider how the sound of the letter *o* changes from one word to another (*pot*, *robe*, *point*, etc.). Now combine the *o* with a *w* and the sound made by *ow* differs from *clown* to *flown*. At best we can instruct the most basic patterns and then, as children read, they will figure out the rest of the relationships between letter patterns and their sounds. David Share (1995) has repeatedly stressed that learning to read is a self-teaching system and that the more students read, the more patterns they will learn. Some children do this effortlessly, while others struggle for several years. The children who struggle will require more phonics instruction for longer periods as they continue to read extensively.

Knowing letter-sound patterns is necessary, but readers also must know what to do with them. They need instruction in the "how to" of reading. What do readers do when they encounter a new word? What strategy might they use? They might try to decode the word moving left to right, letter-by-letter across the word—that is, sound it out (Lovett, Steinbach, and Frijters 2000). They might also look for a part they know and use an analogy to decode the new word. Knowing the word *black* and its rime *ack*, readers should be able to induce the pronunciation of the word *snack*. Or they might first look for prefixes and suffixes—units of language that convey meaning—and then find spelling patterns they know and eventually blend all these units together. Children must also possess some metacognitive skills. They need to decide what strategy to use and avoid using just the initial letter to guess a word's identify. Once they have pronounced the word, they need to instantly judge whether it make sense and if not, correct the mistake (Lovett, Lacerenza, et al. 2000).

Since decoding new words involves the strategic use of language patterns, an important part of phonics instruction takes place while children are reading connected text. Here we can coach children, remind them to apply strategies and rethink miscues. An important part of phonics instruction is learning how to respond to children and how to support their attempts to identify new words. Sometimes children have to read aloud while we take notes. We need to encourage the use of word identification strategies and model them when necessary (Piasta et al. 2009).

What Kinds of Books Support Learning to Read?

As effective teachers and parents already know, children should read books that are engaging, stimulating, and at their reading level. For children who find it relatively easy to learn to read, the structure of the book matters little, they don't need decodable books; think more about content and interests. When strong readers see a new word and successfully decode it, one or two experiences are enough for the word to enter their reading vocabulary.

For children who struggle learning to read, word repetition and decodability are critical, especially the first few months (Juel and Roper-Schneider 1985). Some texts repeat words, and others repeat phonics patterns. The more often readers encounter a word, the more likely they will remember it. If children have been working on short *a* words during their phonics lesson, it is very useful to read a decodable story that contains many short *a* words. These texts provide three advantages. First, the decoding system they are learning makes sense to the children and they can quickly apply in context what they have been practicing in isolation. They gain a sense of control and confidence. Second, decodable texts provide the repetition with phonics patterns that some students require. Decodable texts have more, shorter words than nondecodable text, and the words are repeated more often (Adams 2009). Third, the decodable texts encourage students to move carefully, left to right, across each word, instilling a strategic approach to word identification.

Should Young Readers Be Encouraged to Use Context and Pictures to Identify Words?

Although it may surprise many parents who spend hours reading with their young children and pointing to the pictures, the use of context and pictures can hinder learning to read. Context can assist young readers, but only if they have a firm grasp of letter-sound cues (Tunmer and Chapman 2006). The weakest readers rely on context, because they lack word skills. Ultimately trying to predict or guess words is much less successful than using the letter-sound cues within a word. The most important words in a text—the nouns, verbs, and adjectives—cannot be inferred from the context, but the little function words—*it*, *of*, and *for*—can be predicted. If readers try to guess the meaningful words from context, comprehension will be impaired and vocabulary will be slow to grow. The most disabled readers rely on context because they have such difficulty using the letter-sound cues to identify new words. Depending on context can become a bad habit. When children are reading books— and they must read widely—it is our job to support children's use of phonics to decode new and difficult words and guide them until they become independent word solvers.

Why Do Some Children Struggle with Learning to Read?

Many children come from homes where they are read to often, are exposed to alphabet and rhyming books, play rhyming and other word games, and develop a large vocabulary through their parents' incessant chatter. All these experiences build language skills, the foundation of learning to read. This is *literate cultural capital*. The more multisyllable words children know, the more they are aware of the rhythm in language; from there an awareness of the inner syllabic and phonemic structure of words begins to emerge. Just by learning the names of the letters children have some insight into the respective sounds, since the name of most letters contains its most frequent sound. Letter names give children an edge in learning to spell—*BL* for *bell*, *DG* for *dog*. When listening to alphabet books, especially those that stress alliteration (*six slithering snakes sliding silently southward*), children develop an awareness of initial sounds. Shirley Brice Heath, in a large sociological study (1983/1996), estimated that middle-class children come to school with 1,500 hours of reading instruction, while low-income children experience at best only 50 hours, giving middle-class children a distinct advantage.

Do All Children Need the Same Type of Reading Instruction?

The answer, simply, is no. As we mentioned previously, how children are taught to read depends strongly on the literate cultural capital they bring with them into the classroom. Children from strong language and literate backgrounds benefit from wholistic approaches to instruction. They need to read and write often and require skill instruction only when problems occur. The members of the class without the benefit of preschool and rich language experiences at home need explicit instruction in phonemic awareness and phonics and an incessant exposure to print and reading. Explicit phonics and phonemic awareness instruction provides the insight and the skills that the students did not gain in their home environment (Tunmer, Chapman, and Prochnow 2006; Juel and Minden-Cupp 2000). Whole-group instruction is desirable for all children since through it children develop vocabulary, build an understanding and appreciation of authors and books, build knowledge, and learn to comprehend. Phonemic awareness and phonics must be taught in small, relatively homogeneous groups of children. There is no perfect reading program; all programs must be adapted to the needs of individual children.

CHAPTER 3

Fine-Tune the Whole-Group Lessons in Your Core Reading Program

M s. Miller and her reading coach, Mrs. Mann, are reviewing the next lesson in the third-grade core reading program. Elements taught in the comprehension section include making inferences, questioning, relying on story structure, making judgments, and creating multimedia reports. Word work focuses on the sounds of /oo/ as in *tooth* and *cook*, the suffix *-less*, and using the dictionary. The program also includes a short read-aloud, a historical fiction selection in the student anthology, leveled readers, work on pronouns and exclamations, and the presentation of an oral book report. And school policy is to spend thirty minutes a day on whole-group instruction. Ms. Miller and Mrs. Mann have to make some instructional decisions: what activities should be part of whole-group instruction and what activities should take place during small-group work?

Whole-Group Instruction in Your Core Reading Program

While teaching to the whole class is not an officially stated core reading program position, until very recently core programs provided little direction for differentiating instruction for small groups of students. Differentiation was accomplished by reteaching skills and using additional practice activities. Starting in 2008 core programs added directions for teaching to small groups, but whole-group lessons remained unchanged. The teacher was given more to do, but time did not expand accordingly. With such a wide range of whole-group lessons to choose from—phonemic awareness, phonics, spelling, oral language development, vocabulary words and skills, comprehensions skills and fluency—what are our priorities? What are the benefits of whole-group instruction?

Whole-group instruction should be reserved for activities that will benefit all members of the class and bring them together in a united purpose. If students spend all their time either working at a learning center or meeting in small homogenous groups, teachers send the message that there is no higher purpose to the work, no common goal. Students' being part of a large important project or sharing what they have accomplished individually creates a sense of community and diminishes the stigma that John and Helen are reading a small leveled book while other students are reading short novels. This chapter explores the most important things that should be taught during whole-group instruction and how the focus of that instruction changes with the age and skill of your students.

THIS CHAPTER WILL HELP YOU:
- Use short, engaging drills to build decoding and fluency.
- Build oral language skills through an interactive morning message and other routine activities.
- Read aloud authentic children's literature that builds vocabulary and comprehension.
- Introduce comprehension strategies clearly and explicitly.

What Research Says About Whole- and Small-Group Instruction

The emphasis the core programs place on whole-group instruction stemmed from research that supported the value of direct, explicit instruction, which includes identifying precise goals, breaking skills into small steps, giving clear explanations, and providing the opportunity to practice with systematic corrective feedback (Rosenshine and Stevens 1986). This was the preferred band of instruction twenty-five years ago, but we have modified our views since then. Explicit whole-group instruction is most effective when teaching a well-defined body of knowledge (literary genres, for example), developing vocabulary, or introducing a very explicit skill (using the dictionary, for example). Core reading programs have embraced this body of research. The research is equally clear that small-group instruction is more effective when content or goals are not well defined—engaging in a discussion, applying complex strategies, or analyzing literature, as examples (Rosenshine and Stevens 1986). Since phonics, an explicit skill, is an area in which students have very different abilities, we still find small-group instruction is most effective, although some fast-paced review in whole groups is often desirable.

Activities That Can and Should Take Place in Whole-Group Instruction

• •

Figure 3.1 summarizes our recommendations for how to use your whole-group time. Generally we recommend that you spend thirty to forty-five minutes in whole-group instruction, reserving the bulk of your time for small-group instruction and independent activities.

Whole-group time is useful for introducing reading and writing projects, reading good books aloud, building vocabulary, learning about important authors and books, and introducing comprehension skills and strategies (although the bulk of comprehension development takes place during read-alouds and small-group discussions). Whole-class lessons can also promote oral language development in young children, since weaker language learners benefit from working with stronger students. Phonemic awareness, phonics, and reading fluency are more suited to the small-group setting, because of students' varying ability levels. However, whole-group time is an excellent opportunity for students to review these skills through quick, fast-paced repetition. Review can be continued when students line up for lunch and recess or when getting ready to leave at the end of the day.

Figure 3.1.   What Should Be Taught to the Whole Class

	K	First	Second	Third	Fourth	Fifth
Daily Drill: Reviewing letter sounds, high-frequency words, and phonics	✓	✓				
Developing oral language	✓	✓	✓			
Developing and sharing whole-class projects, authors, and books	✓	✓	✓	✓	✓	✓
Reading aloud to build vocabulary and comprehension	✓	✓	✓	✓	✓	✓
Teaching vocabulary	✓	✓	✓	✓	✓	✓
Initial comprehension skills and strategy instruction			✓	✓	✓	✓

Daily Review of Phonemic Awareness, Phonics, and High-Frequency Words

Ms. Fenwick, a model kindergarten teacher, likes to begin her reading block with a fast-paced drill of skills that have already been taught in small reading groups. Reinforcing phoneme segmentation, letter-sound correspondence, blending, and high-frequency words helps these skills become automatic and frees children to devote most of their energy to comprehension. If these basic skills are not automatic, meaning they require attention and deliberate thought, comprehension will be impaired (LaBerge and Samuels 1974). She keeps a container of flash cards in her meeting area with alphabet letters, decodable words, and sight words the students can review in a three-minute routine. Since it's difficult to individualize this activity, the flash cards can follow the core program's scope and sequence. She maintains high student engagement and ensures maximum focus and participation through every-pupil response—that is, rather than calling on volunteers one by one, having all students answer at once either vocally or by giving a thumbs-up, writing on a whiteboard, or holding up a flash card.

LETTER-SOUND CORRESPONDENCE.   After she introduces the letters and sounds to her kindergarten class, Ms. Fenwick reviews them daily. She first models the activity; then, as her students catch on, she picks up the pace until the routine is quick and seamless. For example:

> We are going to review the letters and the sounds they make. When I hold up a card with a letter on it, we will say the letter sound and then we will say the name of the letter. [She holds up the lettercard *M/m*.] *M* is the name of the letter; it makes the /m/ sound. [Students repeat the name and sound of the letter *m*, and Ms. Fenwick provides feedback by correcting errors and modeling the correct response. Ms. Fenwick holds up another card.] The sound of the letter *t* is /t/. Everyone say /t/.

HIGH-FREQUENCY AND DECODABLE WORDS.   Ms. Fenwick next moves on to high-frequency and decodable words. She says the word, and the students repeat the word. Then she segments each word, holding up one finger for each sound, and the students follow suit. Once each word has been segmented, she and the students blend the sounds back together. Ms. Fenwick scaffolds and supports her students by modeling the activity as often as possible and having the students echo her responses:

Ms. Fenwick: I am going to show you one of our reading words. [She holds up a card containing the word *was*.] This word is *was*. What is the word?

Students: *Was*.

Ms. Fenwick: I am going to say the sounds for each letter. The *w* says /w/, the *a* says /u/, and the *s* says /z/. The word is *was*. Now I will break the sounds apart. My turn, /w/ /u/ /z/, *was*. Your turn.

Students [using fingers to count sounds]**:** /w/ /u/ /z/, *was*.

If kindergartners review these skills daily, they are soon mastered. Continuing the routine drills new students who may join the class during the year. Some of these drills may also be used at the beginning of first grade but then discontinued.

Oral Language Development in the Primary Grades

Oral language is the foundation of reading instruction, and children enter kindergarten with widely different abilities (Hart and Risley 1995). Oral language lessons in a core reading program may include posing a question for students to discuss, reading and discussing a poem, or writing and sharing a morning message. These activities provide a context in which students can build communication skills, especially broadening their vocabulary and sharing and building their knowledge of how language works.

QUESTION OF THE DAY.   Students are seated together on the carpet. On the easel you've written a question connected to the theme of the unit. As children answer and discuss the question, they are developing vocabulary and language skills. For a unit with an animals theme (as in Chapter 2), your question for the day might be *why do dogs make the best pets?* or *why do we need zoos?*

While core programs provide questions like this, they offer no guidelines on how to stimulate oral language development. You want students to speak and elaborate but not all at once. Know your students' verbal abilities and pick no more than three students to respond to the question at first but encourage others of lesser ability to chime in later. Don't always pick the most talkative students. Encourage children to elaborate on short responses and model how to do so. If the question is *why do dogs make the best pets?* and the child responds, "You can play with them," you might model by saying, "That's right, you can play chase or throw a Frisbee for them to catch," and have the student repeat the expanded response. This teacher response validates what the students have said and models a longer response.

HERE'S A SHORT LIST
OF GOOD POETRY FOR
CHILDREN:

- *Sing a Song of Popcorn*, edited by Beatrice Schenk de Regniers et al.
- *A Child's Introduction to Poetry*, by Michael Driscoll
- *The New Kid on the Block*, by Jack Prelutsky
- *Where the Sidewalk Ends*, by Shel Silverstein
- *A Light in the Attic*, by Shel Silverstein

READ AND DISCUSS A POEM.   Reading and discussing a poem is another way to build oral language and prior knowledge. Read the poem and then have your students recite it with you, either line by line or stanza by stanza. (Children who have the necessary skills could then read the poem to the class.) Next, use the poem as the basis for a variety of activities. Start by discussing what the words and images mean. Point out important sensory words and ask what other words convey the same sensations. Then return to the poem and highlight the decodable words, high-frequency words, and spelling patterns the class has been studying.

MORNING MESSAGE.   Most core programs include a daily morning message, a whole-class activity that teaches print awareness, writing, and spelling; reviews phonemic awareness and phonics; and builds prior knowledge. Students have the opportunity to talk and share ideas while expanding their oral language skills. Typically, the core program has the teacher post a partially written message on an easel in front of the classroom. For example:

> [Child's name] is going to _____ with _____ .

The program has the teacher lead a brief discussion about things children can do with their family, asking students to share their thoughts and experiences. Questions to guide the activity include:

- What are some things you do with your family?
- Who can show me where to begin writing?
- Let's count the letters in [child's name]. How many letters are there?
- What letter will I write first in the word *going*?

INTERACTIVE MORNING MESSAGE.   While the core reading program activity above reinforces print awareness, teaches a bit about writing, and develops phonemic awareness, it can be expanded and used to model the writing process and review high-frequency words and phonics principles. The key is making the activity interactive. Engagement should be high throughout (all students should be encouraged to participate), and students should gradually assume more responsibility. Tighten your pacing by having your materials well organized and anticipating the wording of the final message. (The interactive morning message can be used every day in kindergarten and the first few months of first grade and then slowly transformed into an interactive writing activity in grades two and three.) Let's go into Mrs. Fenwick's kindergarten classroom and observe her interactive morning message.

Ms. Fenwick prints the message below on chart paper:

Kindergarten News

Mike is going to _____ for _____ .

She prints the individual words in the headline in different colors to help students focus: *kindergarten* is written in red, *news* is in blue. She also highlights the first letter in the sentence and the period at the end to develop the concepts of beginning and ending.

First, she reads each word in the title to the students while tracking the words with a sweeping motion using her pointer. The students echo her as she says each word:

Ms. Fenwick: *Kindergarten.*

Students: *Kindergarten.*

Ms. Fenwick: *News.*

Students: *News.*

Ms. Fenwick: *Kindergarten* is the red word. What is the red word?

Students: *Kindergarten.*

Ms. Fenwick: *News* is the blue word. What is the blue word?

Students: *News.*

Ms. Fenwick: Let's clap the words *kindergarten news.*

Ms Fenwick and Students: *Kindergarten news.*

Ms. Fenwick: We clapped two times. The heading *kindergarten news* is made up of two words. [She points to the *k* in *kindergarten.*]

The beginning sound in *kindergarten* is /k/. What is the beginning sound?

Students: /K/.

Ms. Fenwick: The letter *k* makes the /k/ sound. What letter makes the /k/ sound?

Students: *K.*

[Ms. Fenwick follows the same procedure for the beginning sound of *news* and the ending sounds of both words until students have mastered these skills.]

The print awareness aspect of an interactive morning message builds students' writing skills. At first you supply a sentence with a few cloze blanks, and the students help you fill in the words. Over time you can begin with an idea or topic, and you and the students write the message while talking about the writing process. The subject of the message might be linked to the read-aloud or the unit project. During the activity the discussion moves back and forth between the process of composing and the mechanics of writing.

For this early fall lesson, Ms. Fenwick tells students they are going to write about Mike's special dinner last night:

> We have a sentence on our paper. A sentence is a group of words that describes something, says something, or asks a question. I am going to touch the first word in the sentence. The first word in a sentence starts on the left [she touches the word *Mike*]. This is the left side of our paper [she touches the left edge of the paper] and we always begin reading at the top of the page [she touches the top of the page]. All sentences begin with a capital letter. The first letter in our sentence in an *M*. I'm going to put a yellow box around the *M* to show that the first letter in a sentence begins with a capital letter. I am going to begin reading the sentence here on the left and move my finger to the right.
>
> I am stopping here at this dot, called a *period*. A period comes at the end of a sentence and tells us to stop. I am going to put a yellow box around the period to show that it comes at the end of a sentence and tells me to stop reading. Now let's go back to the beginning of our sentence, and this time I want you to echo each word that I read.

Notice the lesson is very explicit. At this point you are ready to compose the message. Brainstorm ideas to complete the sentence and then guide the class to a consensus.

Keep this activity short—five or ten minutes. Choose three students each day to respond to the daily message: a student who needs to grow in his oral language; one from a high-ability group, capable of more robust oral language; and a child of average ability. Help weaker students expand their utterances and shape their language skills. When the ideas have been discussed, fill in the responses, but have the students help you.

Ms. Fenwick's message is *Mike is going to his grandfather's house for dinner*. Here's an example of how she models the writing process:

> We are going to write the word *his*; *his* is made up of three sounds, /h/ /i/ /s/. Watch me hold up a finger for each sound you hear in the word *his*. Now, let's do this together and break apart the word *his* with our voices and our fingers. Now I am going to write the word *his* on the paper. I will break it apart with my voice as I write the letters that go with each sound. *His* begins with the /h/ sound. *H* says /h/ so I'm going to write an *h*. After /h/ I hear /i/. The letter *i* makes the sound /i/ so I'm going to write an *i*. The last sound I hear is /z/. The letter *s* makes the sound /z/ in *his*. Now I'm going to put all of the sounds together and blend them to make the word *his*.

Gradually let students take on more responsibility for writing the words, especially as their phonemic awareness and spelling develops. When the entire message has been written, have the students echo read it with you. Over time the cloze sentences become unnecessary; you and the students compose the message together. Continue to use the activity to explain aspects of the writing process like spelling and punctuation. The completed messages can be typed up and sent home for the students to read to their family.

The interactive morning message has many payoffs. As the students learn to compose a message, their oral language skills grow. As they learn to spell words, their decoding improves. After helping create a message, they are excited to take it home to read with their friends and family.

Comprehension Strategies and Skills

The whole-group time is ideal for introducing and providing direct instruction in comprehension skills and strategies. Most students, especially those in the primary grades, need to have comprehension skills and strategies clearly explained and modeled. Students in the upper grades may need to review comprehension skills and strategies at the beginning of the year. You can model strategies while reading aloud to the class; and in small-group guided reading discussions students can practice what they have been taught (Chapter 8 discusses small-group guided comprehension instruction).

According to a wide range of research studies, the essential strategies are predicting and making inferences, determining importance and summarizing, following the structure of narrative and expository text, self-questioning, and monitoring comprehension (Duke and Pearson 2002; National Reading Panel 2000; RAND Reading Study Group 2002). Core reading programs include too many comprehension skills and strategies, leading students and teachers to believe that comprehension requires multiple approaches when just a few well-crafted thinking strategies will serve the reader well (Dewitz, Jones, and Leahy 2009). There is no research supporting the argument that teaching more skills and strategies benefits children. Strive for depth, not breadth.

What's the best way to teach comprehension skills and strategies? Research repeatedly calls for explicit instruction, and evaluations of core reading programs have shown that their lessons are not as explicit as they should be (Miller and Blumenthal 1993; Dewitz, Jones, and Leahy 2009). For good readers, who naturally latch on to the essentials of reading, explicit instruction is not vital. But for average developing readers, especially those who struggle, direct explanation of comprehension *is* vital, because the cognitive mechanisms of reading are largely hidden from view and difficult to pick up (Duffy et al. 1986). Third graders do not naturally know how to find main ideas, determine the theme, or summarize what has been read.

The most effective way to teach comprehension skills and strategies is to:

- Define the skill or strategy clearly.
- Describe the process or procedure for implementing the skill or strategy.
- Tell why the skill or strategy is important.
- Tell when the strategy should be used.
- Model the strategy several times using text of increasing complexity.
- Think aloud while modeling so students gain insight into the comprehension process.

Core reading programs clearly define the skills and strategies in their introductory or review lessons, but after that the quality of their instruction declines in a number of ways (Dewitz, Jones, and Leahy 2009). Some programs do a poor job of helping the teacher explain the underlying mental process. Other programs neglect the *why* of the strategy and fail to give the students a strong motivational purpose for using the strategy. Still others ignore the conditional aspects of the strategy—*when* a reader should use it. Modeling is often limited to a few short examples that do not take into account how the strategy needs to change as the text becomes more complex and demanding.

Our approach to strategy and skill instruction is guided discovery. We want students to work along with us to discover the "secret" underlying the skill or strategy. A discovery-oriented lesson engages students more fully in the process and promotes deeper understanding. This means using many examples of increasing complexity and encouraging students to discover the principles underlying the strategy. Each lesson has four parts: defining the skill; discovering why the strategy is important; discovering the mental process; and learning when to use the skill.

MAKING INFERENCES: A MODEL LESSON.   Making inferences is probably the most important and the most pervasive of reading strategies. At the lowest level, consider this text: *Pam ran to the bus. It pulled away before she could jump on board.* Readers have to infer that the word *it* is a reference to *bus* and *she* to Pam. Of course, most inferences require making much more complex connections than this, often connecting ideas across paragraphs. The most demanding inferences require that readers fill in from prior knowledge what the author only implies. To make an inference readers have to recognize that an inference can or should be made, have the necessary prior knowledge to make the inference, and connect that prior knowledge to the text. That means we can improve children's inferential comprehension by building their prior knowledge, helping them realize when an inference should be made, and showing them how to make an inference. Below is an example of how a lesson might play out.

Define the strategy: Why are inferences important?	Write the following sentence on the board.
	
	    After searching for her scarf and umbrella, Janice gave up and decided not to walk the dog today.
	
	    Lead a discussion of what the author left out of his sentence. Students should be able to note that it was raining and Janice didn't want to get wet. Then point out that inferences are ideas or information the reader adds to a story or article that the author has not included.
	    Now use a more complex example:
	
	Mario was smiling. There were cute little puppies lined up in cages and lots of goldfish swimming around in a huge tank. He could hear birds chirping, kittens meowing, and gerbils running on their little wheels. He had a big decision to make. His dad looked at him, smiled and said, "Well, here we are! Are you ready for your new responsibility?" Mario's heart started beating faster. He was so glad Dad said yes to what he had wanted for so long!

	In this example more than one inference is possible. Begin by asking students what the author has left out. Point out that we can infer where Mario and his Dad are, what decision Mario had to make, and how he felt about it. As you work through the example, keep a list of what can be inferred by the reader—*setting, feelings, causes and effects.* Tell students that reading requires cooperation between the writer and her readers. Often the writer does not tell us everything, and we must fill in what she leaves out.
Discover the process	Give the following paragraph to the students and have them read it: > Mom and Jeffrey raced around the house collecting Jeff's spikes, glove, water bottle, cap, and uniform. His stuff was hard to find because it was still dark outside and they didn't think to turn the lights on. Jeff yawned as he searched every corner of the house. When they finally gathered everything in Jeff's bag, they ran out the door. This was going to be a long day, but Jeffrey was excited! Think aloud for the students: > If I were looking for my spikes, cap, and uniform I might be headed out to play soccer. But a glove isn't used in soccer, although it's essential for baseball. We also know that Jeffrey was excited, so he is probably doing more than just practicing. He might be playing in an important game. I need to read further and confirm my inferences. Tell students that to make these inferences you have to: **1.** Determine that the author has omitted some important information. **2.** Look for clues—important words in the text. **3.** Think about what you already know, your prior knowledge. **4.** Apply what you know from prior knowledge to the text, thus making the inference.

The following chart, found in many core programs, makes the process of making inferences clear:

Clues in the Text	Reader's Prior Knowledge	Inferences

Determine when to use the strategy

Explain that it is our job as readers to identify when an inference should be made, so we have to be alert and decide whether we can add to what the author has written. Then say:

Let's read and listen to this story [a section of Leo Lionni's *Alexander and the Wind-Up Mouse*] and see whether we can spot places where we need to make inferences:

"Help! Help! A mouse!" There was a scream. Then a crash. Cups, saucers, and spoons were flying in all directions. Alexander ran for his hole as fast as his little legs would carry him.

All Alexander wanted was a few crumbs and yet every time they saw him they would scream for help or chase him with a broom.

One day, when there was no one in the house, Alexander heard a squeak in Annie's room. He sneaked in and what did he see? Another mouse. But not an ordinary mouse like himself. Instead of legs it had two little wheels, and on its back there was a key.

"Who are you?" asked Alexander.

This short selection calls for us to make a few important inferences. In the opening scene the author does not tell us who is screaming or why the cups and saucers are flying. Later when Alexander sneaks into Annie's room and sees the strange mouse, the author does not tell us that it is a toy. We can infer that because we have seen toys with wheels and a little motor that helps them drive around.

All comprehension strategy instruction should be approached in a similar way; describing an invisible mental process must be approached carefully. Start by defining the strategy and indicate why it is important. Next, help students uncover the process of using the strategy—how do we find the main idea or construct a summary? Finally, explore when to use the strategy. You can use the examples in your core program, but you will need to supplement them with your own materials so that students can apply the strategy to increasingly sophisticated texts. By slowly increasing the difficulty of the text we are scaffolding the learning. Once the strategies have been introduced to the whole class, students need to apply them. Young readers can apply them during a more sophisticated and engaging read-aloud as you continue to model comprehension thinking. Older students can apply the same strategies during small-group discussion (a topic addressed in Chapter 8).

Reading Aloud to Build Vocabulary and Comprehension

Children who are just learning to read can understand books they cannot yet read, and the books they *can* read don't challenge their comprehension. Therefore they develop most of their comprehension during read-aloud experiences and whole-class discussions. Reading aloud to older students is a way to build their vocabulary (Hickman, Pollard-Durodola, and Vaughn 2004), model the thinking that builds comprehension, and introduce them to new authors and their books. All core programs provide read-aloud activities, but these experiences mostly use short texts written by unknown authors; when authentic literature *is* used, the original illustrations have been deleted (Dewitz et al. 2010). Your school's library is the best resource for read-alouds—the rich world of children's literature.

When you read aloud, we recommend that you pair a fiction and nonfiction book on the same topic (Santoro et al. 2008) and read four books a week. Ideally these books should support the texts (and theme) in the core program. For example, a unit that focuses on Thanksgiving might begin with the informational book *The Pilgrims' First Thanksgiving* (McGovern 1993) and be followed by the story *Gracias, The Thanksgiving Turkey* (Cowley 1996). It's best to choose books that have a number of interesting vocabulary words students are likely to use in their writing and daily discussions and see in their future reading. The books you select should also have some meat to them. They need to have ideas and concepts that are interesting and demand some thinking. Even the easiest children's stories can deal with concepts like envy (*Alexander and the Wind-Up Mouse*, Lionni 1973), deceit (*Doctor De Soto*, Steig 1982) or fear (*Thunder Cake*, Polacco 1997). A good read-aloud lesson should follow guidelines for the scaffolded reading experience (Graves and Graves 2003) and include before-, during-, and after-reading activities.

Prepare the students by introducing the genre, setting a purpose for the reading, and developing the necessary prior knowledge. Then introduce the author and the illustrator and make connections to other books they have written. (This motivates students to read beyond the core program.) Finally, teach the critical vocabulary to support comprehension. But teach only some new vocabulary words before reading, thus giving students the opportunity to infer word meanings from context clues.

During reading, develop students' comprehension by asking a series of well-crafted questions and modeling appropriate strategies. Comprehension questions help students make connections among ideas in the text and with their prior knowledge. Modeling helps students understand how to make inferences, clarify difficult ideas, and summarize what has been read. Good discussions develop students' thinking.

After you have finished reading, help the students transform what they have learned, perhaps by completing a story map or other graphic organizers. Graphic aids focus students' attention on the important ideas in the selection and help students organize what they are learning. Later they might expand the original graphic organizer by linking two paired books. They can also write a summary of the text or collaboratively write a personal or critical response.

Sample Two-Book Read-Aloud for Kindergarten or First Grade

Figure 3.2 is the instructional planner for a read-aloud featuring the nonfiction book *Hold the Anchovies!* (Rotner 1996) and the fiction book *The Princess and the Pizza* (Auch 2003). (Figure 3.8, at the end of the chapter, is a blank version of the form to use in your own planning.) Read and discuss the nonfiction book first because it helps students understand the fiction book. The lesson here is far more extensive than any in a core reading program, and in most cases you will be selecting new books and developing your own lessons.

BEFORE READING THE FIRST BOOK, *HOLD THE ANCHOVIES!*   Begin by having students discuss a time they have eaten pizza. Prompt them with such questions as *Where can you get pizza? Where do you eat pizza? Describe what pizza looks, smells, or tastes like.* Write their responses on a concept chart (see Figure 3.3). This will build the knowledge of students who lack these experiences.

Figure 3.2.   Instructional Planner for a Fiction–Nonfiction Read-Aloud

Texts and Genre	Vocabulary and Prior Knowledge		Other Materials
Hold the Anchovies! (nonfiction) *The Princess and the Pizza* (fiction)	*anchovies* *dough* *wheat* *kernels* *yeast* *ripe* *soil* *conditions* *flavor*	*fragrant* *gracious* *humble* *mutter* *fret* *practical*	Vocabulary picture cards Sequence chart Story structure graphic organizer

Before Reading

Hold the Anchovies!

Discuss pizza: what pizza looks, smells, and tastes like, how to make it.

Discuss the genre and its purpose.

Introduce the vocabulary words accompanied by picture cards.

The Princess and the Pizza

Ask students to recall what they learned from the previous book.

Discuss genre and purpose of the book.

Introduce the vocabulary words by way of picture cards.

During Reading

Read through *Hold the Anchovies!* stopping periodically to discuss important ideas and critical vocabulary. Develop a sequence chart with the students.

Read *The Princess and the Pizza* twice. Clarify story ideas, make and confirm predictions, and relate the story ideas to what the students already know.

After Reading

Use a story structure chart to review *The Princess and the Pizza* and teach the concept of narrative structure. Let the students help complete as much of the chart as they can.

Have the students complete a T-chart comparing the fairy tale with real-life behavior.

Figure 3.3. Concept Chart for *Hold the Anchovies!*

I get pizza from . . .	I eat pizza at . . .	Words that describe pizza
school	home	crunchy
grocery store	school	hot
Italian restaurant	friend's house	cheesy
Chuck E. Cheese	parties	delicious

Next, tell students they are going to listen to a nonfiction book about how pizza is made. Say: "A nonfiction book tells about events, ideas, and people that are real. The author's purpose in this book is to give you information about making a pizza. Before we begin, there are some vocabulary words that we will need to understand." Show the students the vocabulary cards one at a time. Each word should have an accompanying picture that hooks the word's meaning to the students' experiences. Say the word, have students repeat the word, tell students what the word means, and then provide examples and nonexamples of the word. Ask students to try out the word and use it in a sentence. You should teach all the vocabulary words using the same techniques, especially if the words represent new concepts. If the words are new labels for old concepts (*bewilder* for *confuse*, for example), the words require less extensive discussion. For example:

You: This word is *anchovies*. What is the word?

Students: *Anchovies*!

You: Anchovies are small, silvery fish. Here is a picture of anchovies. The picture shows the anchovies in a small can. So we can see that they are indeed a small type of fish. Would you find anchovies in water?

Students: Yes!

You: Would you find anchovies in a forest?

Students: No!

You: Our word is *anchovies*. What is the word?

Students: *Anchovies*!

You: Anchovies are very salty. Sometimes you put them on pizza or on a salad.

Continue to teach the vocabulary words in the same manner, and then develop students' prior knowledge: "On the cover, I see a little girl holding a slice of pizza. She looks very happy, so I think she really likes pizza and knows it will taste delicious. The title of this book is *Hold the Anchovies!* I remember that an anchovy is a small silvery fish. Why would someone hold anchovies? I will have read on to find out more information."

Discuss the basic ingredients of a pizza and how pizzas are made. The students will be familiar with crust, tomato sauce, and cheese, but they will have little idea of how they are made. A K-W-L chart (Ogle 1986) might be a useful instructional tool to capture what the students know and formulate questions.

WHILE READING *HOLD THE ANCHOVIES!* During the reading you have two goals: (1) help the students understand the selection and (2) model strategies that foster comprehension. Read the book aloud, pausing occasionally to discuss the ideas and model how you solved comprehension problems. Stopping too frequently causes students to lose track of the meaning, since they are struggling to build a model of the selection in their heads (Van den Broek and Kremer 2000). The recommendations in *Questioning the Author* (Beck et al. 1997) help students connect ideas within the text and clarify what the author has not made explicit. Figure 3.4 illustrates brief portions of the *Hold the Anchovies!* read-aloud. At each of three stopping points, the teacher asks questions and models thinking.

After reading the text through the first time, complete a sequence chart (see Figure 3.5) to review how to make a pizza and keep notes about the ingredients and the vocabulary. This will help students remember the information and learn the importance of sequence as a concept. As you reread the book ask, "What is the first thing we need for a pizza?" In the notes section of the chart you can clarify the meaning of vocabulary words: "Does anybody remember what dough is and how we make it?"

AFTER READING *HOLD THE ANCHOVIES!* At the conclusion of the lesson have the students design their own pizza recipe or share a response to the book. Very young students can illustrate their pizza; older students can write out the recipe. Students in second grade and up can compare the read-aloud with a nonfiction book they have read on their own. Postreading activities should help students consolidate and organize what they have learned, review strategies that helped them understand the text, and evaluate the text. They need to be geared to the age and ability of your students. The next day you will need to introduce the second book.

Figure 3.4.   Modeling Comprehension Strategies While Reading *Hold the Anchovies!*

Text Segment	Thinking Aloud/Discussion
Pgs. 8–13 Pizza is made from many things. The first is dough. In order to make pizza dough, we need flour. Flour is made from ground-up kernels of wheat. The dough is made by adding warm water and yeast to the flour. The yeast is what makes the dough rise or get bigger. We knead the dough by folding and pushing it with the palms of our hands.	• This book is going to tell me how to make pizza and the ingredients I will need. • How do we make the crust or dough for the pizza shell? • Did the author explain how to make dough? • My summary—making pizza dough is complicated.
Pgs. 16–19 The next thing we need is sauce made from sweet, ripe tomatoes. Tomatoes need sun, clean water, and good soil to grow. To make sauce, the tomatoes need to be chopped and cooked. Spices and herbs add more flavor. The sauce is spread evenly on the dough.	• What is the author describing in this section? • Does the author explain how to make the sauce? • What questions should we ask? • What will we add next to the pizza after the sauce? Lets predict.
Pgs. 20–21 Now comes the cheese. We'll use mozzarella, made with cow's milk. Milk is mixed with an ingredient called rennet, which causes it to thicken. The mixture is heated until it thickens even more and turns into curds. Curds are pressed into balls of cheese. The cheese is grated and sprinkled onto the pizza.	• We were right. Cheese comes next. We used what we knew about pizza and inferred that cheese would be the next ingredient. • Did the author explain how to make cheese? What else do we need to understand? • I don't understand rennet or curd, so I will need to look in another book.

Figure 3.5. Sequence Chart

How to Make a Pizza	What We Learned About Pizza (Notes)
1st	
2nd	
3rd	
4th	
5th	

BEFORE READING THE SECOND BOOK, *THE PRINCESS AND THE PIZZA*.   Begin by focusing on genre, prior knowledge, and purpose. Tell students that today you will be reading them a fairy tale, *The Princess and the Pizza*. Say, "A fairy tale is a make-believe story about a character who faces a problem; often a fairy godmother, elf, or witch plays an important role in the story. The main character is usually able to overcome the problem in order to live happily ever after. The author writes to entertain often teaching his readers a lesson." Remind students of other fairy tales they might know. Tell the students that what they learned yesterday about making a pizza will help them understand this new story. Refer to the sequence chart to help students recall what ingredients they will need to make a pizza. It's most effective if you introduce some of the important vocabulary words before reading the story, pointing out those that were also used in *Hold the Anchovies!* Discuss these words in depth, but leave a few words untaught so students can try to derive their meaning from context.

WHILE READING *THE PRINCESS AND THE PIZZA*.   Read the story twice. The first time, stop to discuss it, pose questions, and explore the feelings and motives of the characters, modeling your thinking when necessary (see Figure 3.6).

During the second reading, focus on vocabulary and author's craft or review difficult interpretations. Begin by asking the students to retell the story. Then reread a few pages and pose questions like these:

- *Clarify story ideas:* "What did it mean when the author said that Paulina's garden barely kept enough food on the table?" (*To clarify story ideas—students should draw the conclusion that she is having difficulty feeding her family.*)

Figure 3.6.   Modeling Comprehension Strategies While Reading *The Princess and the Pizza*

Text Segment	Thinking Aloud/Discussion
Pg. 1 Princess Paulina needed a job. Her father had given up his throne to become a wood-carver and moved them to a humble shack in a neighboring kingdom. Since the king was still learning, his carvings didn't sell, and Paulina's garden barely kept enough food on the table. Paulina missed princessing. She missed walking the peacock in the royal garden, surveying the kingdom from the castle tower, and doing the princess wave in royal processions.	• What is the author telling us about Princess Paulina? • I can infer that Paulina and her dad are going broke and hungry. He is not making money selling carvings and Paulina is not very good at raising vegetables. • How does Paulina feel?
Pg. 2 Paulina tried walking a stray chicken around her shack, but it only pecked at her toes. Surveying the kingdom from the shack's leaky roof made even more holes. She tried princess-waving to the townspeople from her father's cart, but nobody bothered to wave back. They just thought she was swatting flies.	• Given what we know about Paulina, why is she walking the chicken and still princess-waving?

- *Review prior knowledge:* "It says that Paulina tried to make bread by kneading it. Does anyone remember what we learned about kneading from *Hold the Anchovies!*?" (*To review prior knowledge*)

- *Relating old ideas to a new story:* "Paulina squished tomatoes, sprinkled cheese, and put garlic and herbs on top. What did we learn from *Hold the Anchovies!* about making a pizza that helped us understand our new story?" (*To relate old ideas to the new story*)

AFTER READING *THE PRINCESS AND THE PIZZA*.   Discuss the story, and use a story map (see Figure 3.7) to support comprehension and teach the basic story elements. Mapping the story helps students develop an inner sense of narrative and understand story elements such as characters, setting, problem, etc., so they can better comprehend, remember, and retell stories. Eventually students will be able to comprehend and retell a story without the support of the story map.

Extending Your Learning

Study the lessons in your core reading program carefully and decide how you want to supplement them. Here a few things to consider:

- Most teachers start their day working with the whole group. This chapter outlines a number of warm-up review activities. Decide which of them you might use or what others you could create.

- With your grade-level colleagues, go through the read-aloud selections suggested for one of your core reading program themes and identify library books you could use in their place. Consult your school librarian for additional ideas.

- Study some of the skill development lessons in your core program and compare them with the sample lesson in this chapter. Decide how you need to augment the core lessons. *Explaining Reading* (Duffy 2009) is an excellent resource for leaning new ways to teach comprehension skills and strategies.

Further Reading

Duffy, Gerald. 2009. *Explaining Reading*. 2d ed. New York: Guilford.

McCarrier, Andrea, Irene C. Fountas, and Gay Su Pinnell. 1999. *Interactive Writing: How Language and Literacy Come Together*. Portsmouth, NH: Heinemann.

Santoro, L. E., D. J. Chard, L. Howard, and S. K. Baker. 2008. "Making the *Very* Most of Classroom Read-Alouds to Promote Vocabulary and Comprehension." *The Reading Teacher* 61 (5): 396–408.

Figure 3.7. Story Map

Title:	Author:
Genre:	Author's Purpose:
Characters:	
Setting:	
Events:	
Solution:	

Figure 3.8. Instructional Planner for a Fiction–Nonfiction Read-Aloud

Texts and Genre	Vocabulary and Prior Knowledge		Other Materials

Before Reading

During Reading

After Reading

CHAPTER 4

Enhance Your Core's
Word Study Program

At the end of a school year, we all hope our students will have succeeded and met the required standards. The four first-grade teachers working in Lincoln Elementary are no different. This is a rural school with a significant proportion of students from low-income homes; 30 percent of the students are English language learners. Students are assessed at the beginning, middle, and end of the year on several basic word identification skills—letter names, letter sounds, phonemic awareness, spelling, and word recognition. Students making adequate to strong progress are ranked at benchmark level. The students who do poorly are at an intensive level of instruction and are typically given extra instruction—intervention—by a reading specialist. Those with some need are considered to be at a strategic level and the classroom teacher provides the boost they need. At the beginning of the school year Mrs. Paige, Ms. Gonzales, Mr. Turnbull, and Mrs. Akers each had five or six students who needed intensive instruction. When the team sat down at the end of the year with their principal to reflect on results, all were a bit nervous. Mr. Turnbull and Mrs. Akers each had two students still needing intensive instruction; Mrs. Page, who had a master's degree and was completing her seventh year of teaching, now had eleven students at the intensive level; and all the students of Ms. Gonzales, a first-year teacher, were reading at or above grade level. The principal asked the teachers to consider why they had been successful and the sources of their difficulty.

Mrs. Paige, a bit defensive, could not explain her problem. She had taught much as she did in previous years, when she had been successful. She felt that this year's students came from poorer backgrounds, lacked prior knowledge, and had weak language skills. She taught word recognition in whole and small group, saw her four small groups every day for the same length of time, and moved at a slow pace to make sure everyone learned to read.

Ms. Gonzales' answers were much different. She realized early on that her low group was having great difficulty with phonemic awareness and decoding, so she saw that group a second time each day, adding an extra ten minutes, and reduced the time she saw her strongest readers. She knew the low group had difficulty paying attention, so she used puppets (a different one for each child) to lead them through the practice activities. She also incorporated sight word review and decoding practice into other activities—her morning message, reviews of alphabetic order, and learning center games. She even reviewed sight words and decoding while the students waited in line for the bathroom, for lunch, or for afternoon dismissal. She went above and beyond what the core program had suggested.

Word Study in Your Core Reading Program

● ●

A core reading program provides a structure, lessons, and materials for word study. However, most of these resources need to be modified and supplemented to meet the needs of your students. The scope and sequence of skills is appropriate for some students; for others it moves too quickly, with insufficient review; and for the best readers, much of the core program is unnecessary. The teacher's manual provides directions for introducing and practicing phonics patterns and word recognition strategies in lessons primarily intended for the whole class. Some core programs published after 2008 contain differentiated lessons that vary the skills being taught, but even these lessons may need to be modified. A core program also provides decodable and leveled texts for word recognition instruction, but you will need additional books to provide the practice that students require. Finally, a core program provides a wealth of ancillary materials such as word cards, flash cards, letter cards, games, and worksheets. Except for the worksheets, all these materials can be used in your instruction. We recommend very limited use of worksheets or practice books, because research suggests that the more time spent with worksheets, the less students grow in reading ability (Leinhardt, Zigmond, and Cooley 1981).

THIS CHAPTER WILL HELP YOU:

- Organize your students into small groups.
- Sequence and differentiate phonemic awareness and phonics instruction in small groups.
- Select texts that reinforce phonics instruction.
- Use different styles of scaffolded reading to build students' reading accuracy and fluency.
- Coach students how to use word identification strategies.
- Differentiate instruction for struggling readers and English language learners.

What Research Says About Word Study
• •

How we teach word identification skills depends—*depends* being the operative term. Children who enter school with a background rich in literacy seem to grasp the essence of decoding with minimal instruction and benefit from less structured phonics programs (Tunmer and Nicholson 2011). We can support their decoding efforts, explaining and modeling when necessary, while they are reading. Students who enter school lacking these literary experiences require an explicit, code-emphasizing approach that teaches phonics in a precise, sequential way (Juel and Minden-Cupp 2000). The keys to successful word study are teacher knowledge and diagnostic assessment. It has been well documented that the needs of strong readers even in first grade are very different from struggling readers (Connor, Morrison, and Katch 2004). While the suggestions in this chapter focus more on struggling readers, they also address the needs of strong readers.

Organizing Your Small Groups
• •

Many teachers find placing students in small groups daunting; they typically raise these questions:

- How many reading groups should I have?
- How many students should be in each group?
- How do I assign students to groups?
- How long do I meet with each group?
- Will the students in my groups change?

Most reading curriculums allot an hour for small-group instruction. This allows teachers to work with three groups for an average of twenty minutes each or four groups for fifteen minutes each. With more groups the number of students in each group is smaller and the groups are more homogeneous, but the amount of time spent with the teacher is shorter. As the number of reading groups increase, the time students spend working on independent assignments also increases; this is not ideal for the weakest students. The time you spend moving from group to group also eats into your instruction; the more transitions, the more lost time. We advocate having three reading groups and urge teachers to use time flexibly.

The number of students you place in each group depends on their ability. Students working below grade level need intensive attention; group size should not exceed six. Groups working on grade level can have six to eight members, and an above-grade-level group as many as ten. Place students into groups based on reading level, not skills. Students who struggle with reading have any number of problems, so skills-based groups are a narrow and unsatisfactory solution. We would not build a reading group around just one skill such as phonemic awareness or decoding short *a* words. Students who struggle have multiple problems and need instruction in which phonemic awareness, letter-sound associations, and decoding strategies are practiced together. We would not build a reading group around phonemic awareness or decoding short *a* words, since these skills must be taught and practiced together. Reading groups should also be fluid. As students make gains, plateau, or begin to struggle, instruction needs to change to meet their needs; they may need to become part of a different group.

Once you have assigned students to their respective reading groups, decide how long to meet with each group. Struggling readers need more time with you; strong readers need less of your time. They flourish when working alone or with a partner on comprehension-centered activities (Connor et al. 2009). Twenty minutes is a reasonable amount of time for average readers. Plan on twenty-five minutes with your weakest readers (or follow the example of Ms. Gonzales and meet with that group twice). On some days you might see your strongest readers for only five or ten minutes, then let them work independently on a reading/writing project, and briefly review their progress and share their accomplishments at the end of the session. The time not spent with the stronger readers can be shifted to the weakest readers.

Ms. Gonzales began the school year with twenty-seven students in her classroom. With this large a class, she wondered whether she should have three large reading groups or break them into four smaller groups. She knew that if she went from three groups to four, she would have less time for each group. She took into consideration the extra transition time needed to manage four groups and the time students would spend working independently. Her students needed a lot of explicit instruction if they were to be successful; with four groups, she would see her students for only fifteen minutes (give or take) each day. Ms. Gonzales chose to have three groups, knowing she could always see some children twice a day.

Sequencing Phonemic Awareness and Phonics Instruction

• •

Research suggests that students first become aware of words within sentences; then syllables within words; then initial sounds, onsets, and rimes within words. Finally they are able to recognize individual phonemes (Stahl 2001). Many core programs diverge from this sequence and review harder and easier skills each week. On Monday students might listen for initial sounds, on Tuesday detect syllables, an easier skill, and Wednesday segment words into phonemes, a harder skill. Teachers have the authority to modify these sequences to meet the needs of students, especially during small-group instruction.

The introduction of phonics patterns in core programs follows a fixed order, with periodic review. The typical order is individual consonant sounds, short vowel patterns (cvc; ccvc), consonant blends (*bl, str*) and digraphs (*ch, sh, wh, th*), long vowel patterns (cvvc, cvc*e*), and so on. Many of your students may have already mastered the patterns suggested in a given lesson, while others are unable to use patterns introduced weeks ago. The strong readers do not need what the core program offers, and the struggling readers need a great deal of review before moving on. Do some diagnostic work and determine which phonics skills your students have mastered and which they need to know.

Also gauge the needs of your students when planning phonological awareness instruction. All kindergarten students can initially benefit from ten minutes of daily phonemic awareness instruction. By the midpoint of the year on- and above-grade-level students may need only two minutes or less. In first and second grades phonological awareness should be built into the phonics lesson (if it's needed at all). If below-grade-level students cannot yet hear and identify the initial sound in a word, they should not be segmenting and blending a series of phonemes to form a word. Conversely, if you have students in first grade who are reading at the third-grade level, they do not need phonemic awareness instruction. *Phonemic Awareness in Young Children* (Adams et al. 1998) includes effective assessments of children's phonemic awareness skills; also see the Yopp–Singer (1995) test of phonemic segmentation.

Design a sequence of phonics instruction that meets the needs of each group. Start by assessing children's knowledge of the letter-sound patterns and their ability to use that knowledge while reading connected text. Assessments such as spelling inventories (see *Words Their Way*, Bear et al. 2011), the Quick Phonics Screener (Hasbrouck 2006), or a Z-test (McKenna and Stahl 2003) help pinpoint the gaps in students' phonics knowledge. The running record is an important tool for assessing the strategies students use when they encounter a new word while reading; it helps establish how children go about decoding new words (McKenna and Stahl 2003).

Figure 4.1 is a running record of a second grader taken early in the school year. A check mark indicates the word was read correctly and the letter *A* indicates that the teacher assisted the student. A substituted word is simply written into the record. In this running record, John demonstrates that he cannot quite read this beginning second-grade passage; he made nine miscues (the *ate* miscue is only counted once). He could not sound out two-syllable words (*Sebby, everything, problem, Thanksgiving*). His teacher had to provide those words. He also had difficulty with long vowel patterns (*ate, one*).

Introducing Phonics Patterns

Phonics instruction begins by introducing and practicing phonics patterns in isolation. Instruction continues as students read connected text and receive teacher support when decoding new words. The typical weekly core lesson develops letter-sound awareness, introduces phonics patterns, and provides guided practice in decoding and spelling words. Students then read a decodable book and complete phonics worksheets. Sadly, the whole week's phonics activity could be completed in one day. (And if you examine a core program closely, most of the phonics instruction is on Monday and Tuesday.) As teachers, we can do better! To teach phonics well it is important to know how a well-designed phonics lesson is structured (see Figure 4.2). You can apply this structure to any phonics pattern. (Later in this chapter we provide an alternative lesson for struggling readers.)

Figure 4.1. Running Record for a Second Grader

The Text	Running Record
Sebby was a great dog who did almost	✓ ✓ ✓ ✓ ✓ ✓ always
everything right. He came when called. He	A ✓. ✓ come ✓ call. ✓
never ran away. He made his business outside.	✓ ✓ ✓. ✓ mad ✓ ✓ ✓.
Sebby had one little problem; he loved to eat.	Sam ✓ on ✓ pahuh; ✓ ✓ ✓ ✓.
He ate dog food, people food, and everything	✓ eat ✓ ✓, ✓ ✓ ✓ ✓
that fell on the floor. He ate the apple pies for	✓ ✓ ✓ ✓ ✓. ✓ eat ✓ ✓ ✓
Thanksgiving. He ate the candy from	✓. ✓ eat ✓ ✓ ✓
Grandma, he ate cookbooks, and cell phones.	✓, ✓ eat cook, ✓ ✓ pony?

Figure 4.2. Lesson Sequence for Teaching Phonics Patterns

The Lesson Sequence	Teaching Short *a* Patterns
Step 1: Develop phonemic awareness of the target phonics pattern.	Read a list of words, some that have the short *a* sound and others that do not (*can*, *tap*, *man*, *ten*, *tip*, *run*, *fad*). Have the students give a thumbs-up every time they hear the sound. Also ask them if the sound is in the beginning, middle, or end of the word.
Step 2: Connect the printed letter with the sound of the word.	Place six or more short *a* words in a pocket chart. As you point to each word, ask the students what sound the *a* makes. Then slowly decode the word for them.
Step 3. Make words.	In the pocket chart place a number of consonants and the letter *a*. (Students have the same letters or a whiteboard and marker.) Make a word and pronounce it as you do so. Have the students do the same. Have the students read back each word and its spelling.
Step 4: Practice decoding.	Place a decoding chart on the easel with at least fifteen c*v*c words that vary the beginning and ending sounds. Ask the students to read the words aloud as rapidly as they can. Call on individual students to read part of the chart. Be sure to define the words, since vocabulary knowledge aids decoding. {decoding chart below}

can	mat	map	van	lap
sat	ran	hat	nap	bat
fan	rat	tap	man	sap

The Lesson Sequence	Teaching Short *a* Patterns
Step 5: Sort and read words.	With the decoding chart still displayed ask the students to sort the words by ending patterns—*at*, *an*, and *ag*. (They may do the same sort on their whiteboard.) {sort chart below}

at	ap	an
mat	map	can
bat	nap	van
hat	tap	ran
sat	lap	fan
rat	sap	man

The same basic lesson plan can be applied to any phonics pattern. Once the phonics patterns have been introduced and practiced in isolation, through sorting tasks and decoding games, students need to apply what they learned to reading books.

Selecting Texts for Phonics Instruction

Reading skill develops as students apply the phonics patterns and decoding strategies they were taught. Core reading programs do provide leveled and decodable readers, but often there are not enough texts to meet the students' needs. Typically there is only one leveled reader and one decodable book each week (Brenner and Hiebert 2010), so you will have to select additional books carefully. The goal is to get as much text—at the students' instructional reading level—into students' hands and minds as possible. (When reading at their instructional level, students should make no more than five errors for every one hundred words read; O'Connor et al. 2002).

We recommend four leveled or decodable books a week. A decodable book includes words with phonics patterns that have previously been taught. A leveled reader has been ranked in terms of difficulty, number of new words, number of total words, and content. Locate as many resources as possible. Many publishers offer decodable books, and a number of websites offer free, printer-ready decodable books. If your school has a reading room and a literacy coach, check with your coach about possible resources. Use the decodable books first and then switch to leveled readers for the latter part of the week. Figure 4.3 lists resources for decodable books.

How Should Students Read Their Books?

The teacher's edition of the core program typically recommends that strong readers read their stories silently, that on-grade-level students read their stories aloud, and that below-grade-level students do echo or choral reading. These recommendations imply that weaker readers require more support and monitoring than stronger readers do—and also that the core selection is too difficult for weaker readers. Let's assume that you've selected books to match your students' instructional reading levels. How much support do each of these groups really need when they begin to read a new book? How many times should the students read each book? Reading a book, even a short leveled book, poses some challenge even for good readers. You can make the process easier by assessing the difficulty of the text and providing the necessary support.

Figure 4.3. Resources for Decodable Books

Name	Publisher/Website	Free	Purchase
The Reading Genie	www.auburn.edu/academic/education/reading_genie/teacherbooks.html	✓	
Starfall	www.starfall.com/n/N-info/onlinebooks.htm	✓	
Freereading	http://freereading.net/index.php?title=Illustrated_Decodable_fiction_passages	✓	
Ready Readers	Pearson School www.pearsonschool.com/index.cfm		✓
Reading A–Z	www.readinga-z.com/		✓
Bob Books	www.bobbooks.com/		✓
Hubbard's Cupboard	www.hubbardscupboard.org/	✓	

Here's an example. Ms. Heller is introducing the leveled reader *See Me Play* to a below-grade-level first-grade group. She has previously prepared flash cards of words from the book that she anticipates will be difficult—*jump*, *pile*, *must*, *made*, *climb*, and *slide*. These words have either four phonemes or a long vowel pattern. Ms. Heller has her students segment the words while raising a finger for each sound in the words ("Say the sounds in *pile*, /p/ /i/ /l/"), then blend the phonemes back together and pronounce the words ("What word does /m/ /a/ /d/ make?"). She then shows the students the words and they echo and then chorally read each word. Next, she has her students echo-read *See Me Play*, then read it again chorally. The next day the students will reread it two more times, first with a partner, then independently.

How much support students need depends on their reading skills and the difficulty of the text. Always assess the novelty of the concepts and the vocabulary, and preteach concepts and vocabulary new to the students. Sometimes a simple "picture walk" in which you examine and discuss the relevant illustrations is sufficient to build background. Don't fall into the trap that all books require a picture walk; they do not. Some teachers read the entire text to the students before having the students read it. If you are considering this move, you have picked a book that is too difficult, so find an easier book. Nevertheless, a number of rereadings with different degrees of support may be necessary, since this practice builds word knowledge and reading fluency. Keep one thought in mind: the more students read independently, the more progress they will make.

Books can be read in a variety of ways:

- *Echo reading.* You read a sentence and then the students read it back as they point to the words. (A variation: each student reads one sentence and the rest of the students echo it back.)

- *Choral reading.* You and the students read together. If students come to a word they cannot read, the teacher's voice provides support by saying the word correctly.

- *Partner reading.* Pairs of students share the text together and help each other. They may take turns by each reading a sentence, a paragraph, or a page.

- *Whisper reading.* Students read softly and at their own pace as a transition to silent reading. You lean in to monitor accuracy and provide corrective feedback as necessary.

- *Silent reading.* Students read silently. You provide support by conducting prereading activities, setting a purpose for the reading, and prompting discussions along the way. If a student comes to a word he cannot read, he places the finger of one hand on the word and raises his other hand. You can either supply the word or prompt him to use a strategy.

Each group of readers requires a different amount of support. Your goal is always to help the struggling readers achieve independence and not to stifle the strongest readers with unnecessary support. Here are our recommendations:

- Let *above-grade-level* readers read the text silently and independently. They should discuss the book in small groups and reread portions of the text to locate important facts and events, suggest interpretations, and consider the author's craft.

- *On-grade-level* readers should read as much of the text as they can silently and independently. However, some oral partner reading, whether in small-group sessions or while reading independently, will help them build fluency.

- *Below-grade-level* readers may require one or two echo or choral readings. Then they should move on to partner reading or individual reading. You goal is to move this group to independent silent reading.

- *All readers* can benefit from reading a selection a second or third time. For some the second reading builds fluency; others use it to solve comprehension problems; still others gain an appreciation of the author's craft.

Figure 4.4 outlines how you might approach reading with three types of readers. You do not have to work through the entire sequence, but for struggling readers several rereadings are desirable (Kuhn and Stahl 2003). If on-grade-level students are well matched to the book, you might start with some partner reading and then move to silent reading.

We have not mentioned round-robin reading or popcorn reading (a random version of round-robin reading in which students are unable to anticipate who gets the next turn). The problem with either approach is that students read little, are often inattentive, and do not benefit from listening to others read (Opitz and Rasinski 2008). Round-robin reading does

Figure 4.4. Scaffolded Reading Instruction, K–5

Grades K–2

Level of Support	Below-Grade-Level Students	On-Grade-Level Students	Above-Grade-Level Students
High ↑ ↓ Low	Echo reading		
	Partner reading	Echo reading	
	Whisper reading	Partner reading	Partner reading
	Silent reading	Whisper reading	Oral reading to clarify
		Silent reading	Silent reading

Grades 3–5

Level of Support	Below-Grade-Level Students	On-Grade-Level Students	Above-Grade-Level Students
High ↑ ↓ Low	Echo reading		
	Partner reading	Partner reading	Partner reading
	Whisper reading	Whisper reading	
	Silent reading	Silent reading	Silent rereading

provide one benefit: it allows you to listen to students read, make on-the-spot diagnostic assessments, and provide corrective feedback. Echo reading in which the child leads, partner reading, and whisper reading also allow you to listen and provide corrective feedback. Nevertheless, an occasional dose of round-robin reading probably does little harm.

Coaching Students to Apply Word Recognition Strategies

When children are reading they sometimes make mistakes; they *miscue*. Research suggests that identifying new words requires knowledge, strategies, and metacognition (Lovett et al. 2000). Readers must know the phonics patterns. They must have strategies for using the patterns to identify new words, and they must evaluate the results of their efforts and determine whether the word makes sense. Research further suggests that the most successful teachers introduce many approaches to word identification (Piasta et al. 2009). At times they stress sounding out the word, slowly pronouncing the individual letter sounds and blending them together. At other times they may encourage students to look for a word family they know (*at, ick, ope*), break the word into syllables, or use an analogy. If you know *cat* you can figure out *chat*.

As much as possible, you should encourage students to figure out words on their own, modeling strategies and providing corrective feedback. The how and why of corrective feedback depends on the age and ability of the student and the word that is miscued. Students who are very young may not be ready to monitor their own reading and employ strategies independently. They need to be told difficult words, especially those beyond their skill level. Older students should be encouraged to use strategies to figure out words. However, when words are beyond their decoding ability (*soldiers* or *bouquet*, for example) telling them the word is more efficient than applying strategies. You face two important decisions: *how* to respond to the miscue and *when* to respond. Figure 4.5 provides decoding guidance. Refer students to the chart and ask them what strategies they will use to identify a new word. In all cases readers must monitor the results to make sure it makes sense.

Guided reading should be thought of as work, and it's okay to tell students that you're going to do some reading work together (Clay 1993). The child tries to figure out how the letters, sounds, and spelling patterns can be used to pronounce a new word. You provide just the right amount of support, guidance, and hints. What you say depends on the child's

Figure 4.5. Strategies for Decoding Words

Be flexible with vowels,
peel it off, chunk it, rhyme it, sound it out:
thread → bead   or   thread → head

Peel it off - prefixes and suffixes,
chunk it, rhyme it, sound it out:
unfortunately — un-fortunate-ly

Chunk it, rhyme it, sound it out:
refreshments —
re / fresh / ments

Rhyme it, sound it out:
prevent
he / went

Sound it out:
clam
c l a m

Which strategies should I use?

Does it make sense?

Based on Lovett, Lacerenza, and Borden 2000

reading ability and the difficulty of the word. When a child makes a mistake during reading, deal with the problem right after he or she finishes that portion of the text.

Figure 4.6 is a general set of guidelines for corrective feedback that tells you what to do when a student has difficulty. In all cases you should take notes. Have large index cards or a whiteboard at hand so you can write the words the child says and the words she is trying to read. Share both words and focus her attention on the word she is trying to decode.

Figure 4.6. Coaching Students to Identify Words

What the Child Does	What You Say
Miscues a word and self-corrects	When the child is finished reading, praise the self-correction. Tell him that good readers often self-correct. Ask, "How did you figure out the word?"
Miscues, pauses, but does not self-correct	If the child is a beginning first grader, tell him the correct word and have him repeat it, especially if the word is critical to understanding the passage. If the child is a bit older, when she finishes reading, go back to the miscued words and ask, "How could you have figured it out? What strategy might you use?"
Miscues and reads on to the end of the sentence without noticing the miscue	When the child has finished his portion of the reading say, "You made a mistake on that page [in that sentence]. Can you find it?" If that does not work, reread the sentence as he did, with the miscue. Ask, "Does that make sense? Does that sound right?" Then ask, "How could you have figured it out? What strategy might you use?"
Encounters a word he should be able to decode and will not attempt it or decodes it very poorly	Ask, "How could you have figured it out? What strategy might you use?" If the word has one or more spelling patterns the child should know, coach him through the word and use your decoding chart. If the word does not have a known spelling pattern, have the child sound it out with your help.
Encounters a word she should not be able to decode and simply cannot move on	Supply the word.

Figure 4.7 illustrates how you might apply these feedback principles while assisting a first grader (or any student, for that matter). In many cases you are attempting to break bad habits like looking at the first letter and guessing, as well as help the child learn new habits.

It's also a good idea to extend and reinforce strategies students have used. Marie Clay (1993) calls this *cross-checking*. Ask questions about how they figured out difficult words or why they made the corrections they did:

Figure 4.7.   Coaching a First Grader to Apply Decoding Strategies

Text	After Reading
✓ ✓ ✓ ✓ ✓ ✓ ✓ It was a brisk and cloudless April everything✓ ✓ ✓ ✓ ✓ evening. The guests had gathered in ✓ ✓ ✓ ✓ ✓ ✓ ✓ the Red Room, and the table looked ✓ ✓ ✓ ✓ ✓ perks elegant, as even small dinner parties ✓ ✓ ✓ ✓ ✓ ✓ at the White House can be.	• "You made a mistake in the first sentence of this paragraph. Can you find it?" The child does not see the error. You read the sentence with the miscue: "*It was a brisk and cloudless April everything.* Does that make sense?" Ask the student to find the difficult word. The child points to *evening.* • "Can you chunk the word? Are there chunks or parts that you know?" • Point to the other word the child missed and ask, "Does this word have a spelling pattern you know? Let's look at the word family wall." The child sees the key word *cart* and says, "I see *cart* so this word is parties."

- "How did you figure out the word? What strategies did you use?"
- "What parts in the word helped you figure it out?"
- Ask students to compare the word they pronounced with a word in the text and ask, "How did you know it was *parties* and not *perks*?"
- "When you read [*repeat the sentence as the child read it*], what made you go back and read it again?

If children can describe how they identified a new word, we may assume they are taking some strategic control of their reading.

Teaching High-Frequency Words to All Students

High-frequency words are the most common words in English, and children can make little progress learning to read without knowing them well. This is vital for all children. High-frequency words include function words like *the*, *so*, and *of*, and common content words like *girl*, *red*, and *big*. Some high-frequency words have regular letter-sound correspondence (*then, it, she, can*), but others do not (*was, there, said*). All core programs include a basic set of high-frequency words in their kindergarten and first-grade instruction, and these words appear in the core reading selections.

How core programs approach the teaching of high-frequency words varies. Some introduce the words in context; others do not. Some programs stress the meaning and usage of the words; others do not. All programs have the students pronounce the words after they are introduced, and some have them spell the words aloud as well. All programs include daily review activities in which the students recite words that have been placed on a word wall. You can make these lessons more effective by adding a few simple steps. Remember, the more students know about a word, the better they will remember it. A lesson on high-frequency words should include segmenting the sounds in the word, spelling the word, and exploring its function in a sentence (conjunction, preposition) as well as its meaning. In other words, teaching high-frequency words involves more than rote recitation. Here are a few ways a lesson might proceed:

- Introduce three to six high-frequency words per week by writing the words in sentences or a short story. Underline or color code the words.

- Segment and blend the sounds in the words. Even though some words are not phonetically regular, all contain a sequence of phonemes. ("I am going to say this word very slowly and when I am finished, I will say the word quickly. Listen, /h/ /a/ /v/, my word is *have*; /w/ /er/, my word is *were*.") Students should echo and repeat the segmenting with you. Then have the students segment and blend the words without your support.

- Write the words on a whiteboard and carefully spell the words as you do so. ("I am going to write down and read the words we just practiced. The first word is *have*. *Have* is spelled h-a-v-e [*write down each letter*]. The *h* says /h/, the *a* says /a/, and the *v* says /v/. The *e* doesn't say anything. The word is *have*. What is the word?") Then have the students write the words three times on either their whiteboards or a piece of notebook paper.

- Prepare word charts with high-frequency words printed on them:

of	you	is	saw	their
was	said	does	were	have

Have students whisper-read the words. Tell them that if they come to a word they cannot read, they should put a finger of one hand on the word and raise their other hand. Tell the student the word and ask the student to repeat it. When everyone is finished have the students take turns reading the words from the chart while the other students in the group echo the reader.

- If your core program includes stories that stress a set of high-frequency words, read these books with your students. Or construct your own language experience story that features a set of high-frequency words and have the students practice reading it.

Word Study for Struggling Readers

Some children find it difficult to grasp the alphabetic principle that underlies English. They struggle to learn letter-sound associations and cannot implement a decoding strategy when they encounter new words. As a result, their reading vocabulary and reading ability do not grow. These students need intervention. Although core programs offer many reteaching options for these students and some provide small-group intervention lessons, few of these supplemental efforts tackle the decoding strategies these students lack or the metacognitive insights they require. Struggling readers need to select and implement the right decoding strategy and learn to evaluate the results of their efforts. Strategic word identification leads to automatic word identification. Research (Gaskins et al. 1991; Lovett et al. 2000) consistently points out that students who are weak in decoding lack:

- Phonemic awareness
- Knowledge of phonics patterns
- Strategies for decoding words and monitoring word recognition efforts.

Decoding by analogy is a successful approach for working with struggling readers (Gaskins et al. 1991). Teach students three to five key words a week, each key word representing a frequent spelling pattern in the language (*c__at__*, *p__ig__*, *c__an__*, *h__er__*, *w__ent__*). If readers know *can*, they should be able to pronounce *plan* or *bran*. Knowing *car* and *went*, readers can identify *garment*. Week after week students learn new key words and apply their knowledge of spelling patterns to identify new words. When you introduce a key word, explore the

Figure 4.8. A Sample Word Wall for Decoding by Analogy

a	e	i	o	u
c<u>at</u>	t<u>en</u>	p<u>ig</u>	p<u>ot</u>	b<u>ug</u>
c<u>an</u>	l<u>et</u>	w<u>ill</u>	cl<u>ock</u>	f<u>un</u>
m<u>ade</u>	n<u>est</u>	wr<u>ite</u>	f<u>or</u>	tr<u>uck</u>
m<u>ake</u>		sm<u>ile</u>	c<u>old</u>	

sound and spelling of the word and work on rhyming, segmenting, and blending. A word wall organized by spelling patterns (see Figure 4.8) helps students remember the key words and their spelling patterns.

Have students use the spelling patterns and the analogy strategy every day to read words in isolation and in context. They should also use the word wall to spell new words ("If you can spell *cat*, you can spell *chat*"). Then they can apply the analogy approach when reading connected prose. When they encounter a new word encourage them to segment the word, look for known spelling patterns, consult the word wall, and use what they know to pronounce the word. Students need to read extensively in order to practice decoding by analogy.

This approach is an example of an interactive strategy (Scanlon and Anderson 2010). It is not the program that makes the difference but your support, modeling, and problem solving. You must set high expectations for your students and keep them actively engaged through well-paced lessons. Intervention instruction students receive from a reading specialist must be congruent with your classroom instruction—apply the same skills and use the same strategies.

Word Study for English Language Learners

English language learners (ELLs) must learn the process of decoding words and at the same time develop their oral language skills. Research has consistently documented that the best instructional practices for English-speaking students also work for ELLs. However, it is important to integrate strong decoding instruction with these practices. Keep these basic principles in mind:

- Strive for very explicit instruction. English language learners need clear, precise steps to follow, like those on page 79. Begin with a clear statement of the goal. List the steps a student should follow to decode a new word and employ explicit language markers—*first, second, next, last*. Use very consistent language. If you are working on phoneme segmentation, use just the words *separate sounds*; avoid synonymous terms like *segment* and *stretch*. Support these instructional steps with visual markers like holding up an additional finger as each sound in a word is pronounced.

- Embed vocabulary discussions in all you do. When students are decoding a new word, always explain its meaning. If students are working on *am* as in *jam*, explain that jam is like jelly and we spread it on bread and that when we get stuck in traffic we are in a traffic jam. Focusing on multiple meanings helps deepen students' language skills; they learn that words take on new meanings in different contexts. Always discuss the differences between similar words such as *scared*, *frightened*, and *terrified*. These language lessons do not stand alone; effective teachers regularly explain word meanings and usage during a decoding lesson.

- Make grammar explicit. Consistently explain how words are used. If students are attempting to decode the word *can*, illustrate how this word can be used both as a noun and as a verb. *We can throw the ball. We need a can of tuna.*

- Provide ample opportunities for practice. Make sure there are many words to decode in a lesson; come prepared with extensive lists (double what the core program provides). Use every-pupil response as much as possible, so students are not waiting for their turn. Writing on a whiteboard or holding up a flash card representing a spoken word or sound lets each student respond and lets you instantly determine who understands the concept or process.

Independent Work for All Readers

When you are working with a small group, the other class members need to be working on meaningful activities that build their reading skill and interest. Independent work can accomplish this goal if you follow these guidelines:

- The primary activity during independent work should be reading books or articles and writing for real reasons. Ask yourself, *Is what I am asking the students to do more important than reading a book?*

- Specific skill activities should complement what the students are learning in their small groups. This will reinforce what you are teaching. Follow-up activities should stress phonics, fluency, vocabulary, and comprehension.

- Students should understand why they are completing the assignments and be able to tell an adult why if asked.

- Students need to be able to read the directions independently in order to understand the task.

- Activities should not involve cutting and gluing but reading prose and writing for real audiences.

- Independent work needs to be differentiated. Everyone in the class should not be working on the same activity.

- Independent work requires accountability to keep students on task; create assignments that provide feedback.

Workbooks

Core reading programs include a large variety of consumable workbooks in which students practice and reinforce the skills they have been taught. The newest programs provide materials for learning stations. These workbooks and materials come in versions for English language learners and students working below grade level, on grade level, and above grade level. Research on workbooks and worksheets generally paints a grim picture. The more time students spend completing worksheets, even well-designed ones, the less they grow in reading ability. Worksheets replace reading connected text, the most valuable activity (Leinhardt, Zigmond, and Cooley 1981). If you use workbooks at all, follow these criteria (Osborn 1984):

- Tasks should directly relate to instruction presented to the whole class or the small group.

- Tasks should reflect the most important skills and strategies. (For example, focus on vocabulary before extensive drill on punctuation.)

- Only students who need extra practice need the activities.

- The language should be consistent with that used in your small-group lesson. Students must be able to read the workbook, and the directions must be clear and easy to follow.

- The workbook task must have enough to do so that students actually learn something. Volume matters.

- Some of the tasks should be fun and have an obvious payoff (word games and puzzles).

Learning Centers

When some students are working with you, others can be working at their desks or at a learning center. A learning center is simply a place in the classroom that contains a set of activities and the materials necessary to complete those activities. The best centers encourage students to explore, observe, read, and write. There is nothing magical about the learning center approach. The best centers offer students exciting meaningful activities; the worst are nothing more than worksheets dressed up with color coding and lamination. Centers work best when children are familiar with the routines of the center and the routines are not changed very often. Keep the number of centers small and the routine simple. Reading and writing should be the most important tasks for all students. We recommend the following centers:

- Reading center or library where readers respond to what they read.

- Fluency/readers theatre center.

- Word discovery center.

- Listening center.

- Writing center.

READING CENTER OR LIBRARY.   A well-stocked, inviting classroom library is key to a successful reading program. The library needs an abundance of leveled texts, both expository and narrative. It should be organized by level and genre. Book levels can be indicated by dots on the spine in various colors, or leveled books can be stored in color-coded bins. Students should be expected to read a certain number of books per week (in various genres). For texts selected and read, students should fill out a graphic organizer, write a report, or outline an oral report. Students can also reread a leveled text independently or with a partner. The texts can be tied to the theme of what the class is learning and build on the knowledge gained in small reading groups. You could prepare a set of questions for students to answer after they have reread the book.

FLUENCY/READERS THEATER CENTER.   This center provide activities and resources that build students' oral reading fluency. It is appropriate for midyear first graders and second through fifth graders. To increase rate, accuracy, and *prosody* (reading with expression), students can reread a short piece of text several times and chart the change in reading rate and accuracy. Charting their growth provides motivation, since students are excited to see how they are improving.

The goal of readers theatre is to practice a script for a performance later in the week. The practice fosters increased fluency. Students begin by reading a short play or poem during small-group instruction with your support. The play is discussed to build comprehension. Then, in the center, students work together to improve their fluency and present a dramatic reading. They practice their piece in an area that will not disturb their peers but eventually perform it for the class. The performance provides the motivation. (We explain these activities in detail in the next chapter.)

WORD DISCOVERY CENTER.   Here students practice what they are learning about words. Word games expand what they know about words and make their knowledge more automatic. Card and dice games help them build words from word parts—letters, spelling patterns, word roots, prefixes, and suffixes. Constructing and solving crossword puzzles helps them link words to meaning (see *Getting Ready to Read* [Fitzpatrick, Cernek, and Tom 2002] for phonics and phonemic awareness games).

Word sorts enable students to review word patterns previously taught in small reading groups. There are three types of word sorts: an open sort, a closed sort, and a speed sort. A closed sort is the easiest; students sort the words into preset categories: by word family, vowel team, or parts of speech. In an open sort, students create their own categories and explain how and why they sorted the words as they did. In a speed sort, students complete an open or closed sort while being timed. Whatever the kind of sort, students should read the words to a partner and then write sentences using some of the words. For younger students, pictures can also be sorted to match the words. (See *Words Their Way* (Bear et al. 2011) and *Word Journeys* (Ganske 2006). Both of these books provide resources for word games.)

LISTENING CENTER.   This center is appropriate for kindergarten and first grade. Core reading programs for these grades often include CDs of the program's big books being read aloud. After you have read a big book aloud, students can listen to the story again on the CD and follow along in the book. They can also listen to other stories. Listening to stories again and again, students are exposed to proficient reading. At the beginning of kindergarten, the accountability piece could be a drawing of the student's favorite part of the story. As the year progresses, students will begin to draw *and* write their favorite part of the story. Eventually, they can fill out a graphic organizer on story elements or nonfiction facts.

WRITING CENTER.   A writing center contains writing materials—paper, pencils, markers, crayons, dictionaries, and a thesaurus. A writing center might also contain resource books: books on poetry or folktales, style manuals, and punctuation guides. A folder of graphic organizers provides tools for planning and organizing a composition. Samples of other children's writing provide examples and support. Children use the center to complete writing that you assign or that they initiate themselves. If you assign a written response to a new book, the writing center needs to include the tools the students need. If the class is deep into a poetry unit, poetry books in the writing center are the models students consult when they create their own poems.

Summing It Up

The goal of phonics instruction and word study is to help all students become independent readers—to give them the knowledge and strategies they need to teach themselves the new words they encounter while reading. For many children this comes easily. For others it takes a great deal of instruction: phonics patterns may need to be taught explicitly, strategies may need to be modeled, and children may need to be guided to use these strategies. Some students acquire this self-teaching ability in several months; for others it may take several years. Some students require very explicit instruction and coaching; others do not. Key for all students is the opportunity to read extensively and practice their skills. We explore independent reading and fluency more extensively in the next chapter.

Extending Your Learning

- As a grade-level team, organize your classes into small groups. See how your grouping decisions change as you consider different types of data about your students.

- Read through the phonemic awareness lesson of one theme in your core reading program. See if those lessons follow the sequence we outlined on page 79. If the core sequence is not developmental, how might you change it?

- Examine a phonics lesson in your core reading program and compare it with the sample phonics lesson in Figure 4.2. How might you modify the phonics lesson in your core reader? Decide for which group this phonics lesson is appropriate.

- Record a student reading aloud and share the recording (and the text) with your colleagues. Decide how you might respond to the student's miscues.

- Browse the independent activities and the workbooks provided in your core reading program. Which of these activities match the criteria outlined on pages 91–93?

Further Reading

Cunningham, Patricia. 2005. *Phonics They Use: Words for Reading and Writing*. New York: Pearson. (emphasizes decoding by analogy)

Beck, Isabel. 2006. *Making Sense of Phonics*. New York: Guilford. (focuses on synthetic phonics)

CHAPTER 5

Add Independent Reading
and Small-Group Intervention
to Build Fluency

Three second-grade teachers at Elmhurst Elementary are meeting with their literacy coach because many students are not developing solid oral reading fluency and the teachers are looking for direction. The students have recently been assessed for reading fluency via a one-minute timed reading from *Dynamic Indicators of Basic Early Literacy Skills* (Good and Kaminski 2005), a test recommended by the school's core program. The desired benchmark score for the middle of the year is seventy-two words correct per minute. Figure 5.1 shows the results of the test. Of the seventy students in second grade only forty-two meet the target score; twenty-eight students need reinforcement in fluency.

The three second-grade teachers meet with their literacy coach, Mrs. Farschman, to explore solutions. Mrs. Farschman asks the teachers to share their fluency-related instructional practices. Mrs. Johnston drills the Fry sight words for ten minutes each day. Her students spend another ten minutes a day practicing their weekly spelling words for the test on Friday. They also read the main story from the core reader, spending about two weeks on each story. Mr. Allen and Ms. Price follow the same instructional procedures, but they also use decodable and leveled books during small-group instruction. Students reread the books to develop fluency. Overall, the teachers are unsure how to build fluency but are open to any ideas that Mrs. Farschman may have.

Mrs. Farschman realizes that some of these practices are not the most effective and that part of the problem may be tying all the instruction to the core reading program. She suggests that the teachers continue to teach the Fry words (but for no more than five minutes) and that they replace some of their current instructional strategies with ones explored in this chapter.

Figure 5.1. Fluency Ratings for Elmhurst Elementary School's Second Graders

Words Correct per Minute	Percentile Rank	Number of Students
125	90th	7
100	75th	10
72	50th	25
42	25th	16
18	10th	12

THIS CHAPTER WILL HELP YOU:

• Recognize the importance of fluency in developing strong readers.

• Understand the principles underlying the success of independent reading.

• Incorporate independent reading into a core program as a way to build fluency and develop knowledge.

• Incorporate teacher- and student-assisted fluency routines into your reading instruction.

Fluency Instruction in Your Core Reading Program

Until recently fluency did not play a large part in core reading programs. Programs occasionally suggested that students reread selections from the student anthology in order to build fluency, and some suggested activities like partner reading or readers theater. Fluency instruction lacked the thoroughness applied to teaching phonics. However, because fluency has become a central concern of researchers and is stressed as one of the five components of reading in the National Reading Panel report (2000), core programs began featuring fluency instruction more prominently starting in 2005. Lessons on the components of fluency—speed, accuracy, and prosody (expression, phrasing, and intonation)—have been added to core programs and new materials created. A typical brief fluency activity is having students reread a portion of the story in the student anthology. A large stand-alone lesson may require the teacher to explain and model the role of punctuation and phrasing in fluent reading and have the students echo the modeled reading. All core programs have added the assessment of fluency through one-minute oral readings: children read a passage aloud for one minute, and the number of words read correctly is their score.

Even though the role of fluency has become more important in the newer core reading programs, one of the most important means of building fluency is still given short shrift:

reading fiction and nonfiction widely and deeply. Researchers have questioned whether any core program includes enough reading for students to become fluent readers (Brenner and Hiebert 2010). In most programs independent reading takes place just one day a week, typically Friday. (Our sample core lesson in Chapter 2 includes independent reading only on Friday to emulate the typical core program.)

Core programs ignore independent reading for two reasons. First, they want you to believe that all you need to teach your students to read is contained within the program. Second, core publishers do not sell the thousands of trade books that children need to become fluent—the novels, picture books, and information books that fill schools and class-room libraries and are bought by the general public. However, we believe that independent reading has to be included in any comprehensive reading program. It plays a critical role in a student's development of both fluency and comprehension and is now recommended by the Common Core State Standards.

What Research Says About How Children Become Fluent Readers

Fluency is essential for reading comprehension—fluent readers can focus on meaning because word recognition is automatic and requires little attention. Jeanne Chall (1983), an eminent reading researcher, developed a widely accepted stage theory of reading development. In the first stage, preschool and kindergarten, students build their oral language skills and learn some basic principles of reading—print stands for meaning, books contain stories and information, and we read left to right. In the second stage, essentially first grade, children learn the alphabetic principle that letters represent sounds, as well as basic letter-sound correspondence. By the second and third grades, readers should be in the third stage, refining their phonics skills and becoming fluent. In the remaining three stages, readers develop and refine their comprehension and thinking. Chall's stages help us determine which aspects of reading to focus on at what age.

Fluency develops in two compatible ways. Most children become fluent readers by reading widely and deeply. At some point in their literary history they latch on to books. They read series like R. L. Stine's Goosebumps, Ann M. Martin's The Baby-Sitters Club, or Jeff Kinney's Diary of a Wimpy Kid. Series books are easy, and ease is essential for building fluency (Allington 2006). Through the act of avid reading, skills are refined, knowledge builds, vocabulary grows, and comprehension deepens. Children then move out into the wider world of fantasy, science fiction, historical fiction, adventure, and nonfiction.

The other route to fluency is the repeated reading of short text supported and monitored by a teacher, an aide, a parent, or a peer. S. Jay Samuels (1979) introduced this approach with an article, "The Method of Repeated Readings." Children read short passages several times, and their reading rates are timed and recorded on graphs as they strive toward a goal. Samuels and others (Rasinski 2006, for example) have demonstrated that fluency and comprehension can be improved through repeated practice on short passages. Since this initial finding, educators have created variations of this activity; in one, children participate in paired repeated readings (Koskinen and Blum 1986). Publishers have created programs and material for fluency practice, some of which incorporate voice-activated computer software that records students' reading times and errors.

However, when wide reading is compared with scaffolded repeated readings, the nod goes to wide reading. Wide reading exposes students to more ideas and more words. It is through broad independent reading that students make the most progress in developing their fluency and their comprehension (Manning, Lewis, and Lewis 2010).

The First Road to Fluency: Independent Reading

Independent reading is a time set aside in which students select books, read them with enjoyment, and share their responses orally or in writing. A growing body of evidence supports silent independent reading, especially for struggling readers and English language learners (Manning, Lewis, and Lewis 2010). A specific time for independent reading is less critical for strong readers, who already read on their own in school and out. When students are given opportunities to select text that appeals to their own interests, they will very likely do more reading and, in turn, become fluent readers. For independent reading to be successful, students need time, materials, motivation, and choice. It is also important that teachers hold students accountable for their reading.

Time Management

Independent reading can take place during a designated time, as in Sustained Silent Reading (SSR) or Drop Everything and Read (DEAR), or it can be incorporated into your small-group rotation, with all students spending some time reading independently in the classroom library. If your reading/literacy instructional schedule allows, a designated time, perhaps right after lunch or just before dismissal, in which everyone reads silently, without interruption, is desirable. Duration will vary, depending on students' age and ability. Typically, we recommend five or ten minutes for primary-grade students and fifteen or twenty minutes for older students. In the past teachers were told they should model this silent reading, but we think your time is better used in other ways. Students know that teachers read; your job is to encourage, guide, and monitor students' reading. While students are reading, you can conduct individual reading conferences in which you assess and encourage their efforts.

If time constraints preclude the whole-class approach, you can include independent reading in your daily small-group rotations as we suggested in the previous chapter. While you are conducting small-group instruction, one center option for students is reading independently. You will still need to have conferences with students to guide and support them, and the concluding minutes of the reading block are a good time to do so.

Materials

Core reading programs include very few materials for independent reading. Some programs provide a few novels or paperback trade books, but most of your resources will come from your school and classroom library or the book room. These authentic texts motivate students by being interesting and exciting, and they extend students' knowledge and vocabulary. A successful independent reading program requires a well-organized and well-stocked classroom library, six to ten selections per student. Students need to be able to choose from a variety of fiction, nonfiction, magazines, poems, and rhymes. You need to find out what students enjoy reading and coordinate these interests with the themes of the core program. If a unit theme is animal families, for example, bring in twenty or so books on animals from the school library so students can learn more about them.

Students need to select the right books if independent reading is to be successful, and struggling readers often select books that are too difficult (Donovan, Smolkin, and Lomax 2000). This means you need to level books and teach students to select books from a certain level. You could use a system of colored dots to help you. Place a colored sticker on the spine or front cover of a book that corresponds with your difficulty-level color code. Or you can place books in different-colored plastic bins and tell students which bin to select from. Whatever system you use, teach students the three-finger or five-finger rule. Tell primary students that when choosing a book they are to hold up one finger for every word on a page that is difficult. When they get to three fingers, they should put the book aside and find another. The rule switches to five fingers in the intermediate grades.

Motivation

Motivating students to read can be challenging. Some students do not want to pick up a book even under threat of taking away recess for the rest of the year. They have had so few positive experiences with books that reading presents not reward but the likelihood of frustration. The keys to motivation are knowledge, choice, and personal support. The more you and your students know about books, the more they will be motivated to read. To be turned on to a book, students need to know that it might be exciting, that the author is trustworthy, and that their friends Bill and Elaine have read it and liked it. Here are some ways you can motivate your students:

- Share favorite children's books and children's authors with your students daily.
- Conduct author studies. Over a series of weeks read and discuss the work of one well-known author who has written a number of books. Avoid authors who are one-hit wonders.
- When you read a "big book" aloud, make smaller copies available for students to read along with you.
- Read a particularly interesting section of a book to whet students' appetite.
- Have students share what they are reading.
- Encourage your librarian to conduct book talks.
- Show a video of students in other classes (or another school) presenting book reviews of their favorite books, and have copies of the books available to be checked out of your classroom or school library.
- Keep a "bestseller" list in your room of favorite books. Encourage students to add titles they have read to the list and provide a brief rating.
- If you want to reward the amount of reading students do, reward the number of different genres, not the number of pages, books, or minutes (Fawson et al. 2009). All students can read twelve different genres in a semester. Figure 5.2 is a graphic organizer students can use to keep track of the genres they read. The goal is to read one book from each genre each semester, filling in the titles as they go.

Choice

Choice is key to motivation. Adults choose books out of interest or need (unless we are stuck in a suffocating book club and lack the nerve to quit!). Children are no different; they relish

Figure 5.2. A Genre Wheel for Guiding Independent Reading

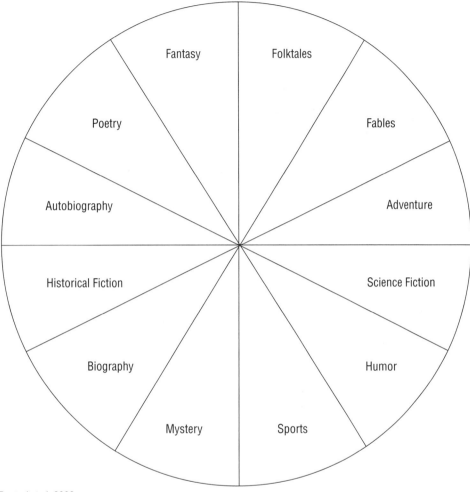

Reutzel et al. 2008

choice and they like what they like. Choice does not require hundreds or even dozens of books. Three books vividly described offer an adequate choice. Students are still in control and that spurs their motivation. The youngest readers require restricted choices; as students get older the range should expand.

Support

Personal support is also an important component of motivation. Avid readers seek out other readers. Many children learn about books from their parents, the librarian, and (perhaps most important) their peers. But children who do not live in a culture of books do not have the experience of listening to others talk about books and reading.

Individual reading conferences are essential for all students, especially those who are not motivated to read. Your friendship and trust are a source of motivation. During two- or three-minute reading conferences you can check on the progress students are making with their book, encourage them to read more, and help them solve comprehension problems. You can evaluate their decoding and comprehension skills and suggest a book for them to read next. Figure 5.3 is a form you can use to guide and document your reading conferences. You can evaluate the student's interest, spur on her motivation, informally assess her comprehension (for younger readers, you might also take a short running record), and help her set goals and pick the next book.

Structuring Independent Reading with Book Clubs
••

Book clubs promote independent reading, fluency, comprehension, and writing through structured discussions and sharing. They are easily added to core program routines and in years past some core programs included them. The natural spot for a book club is during independent reading; alternatively, a portion of class time can be set aside for book clubs two days a week.

Book clubs have both a direct and an indirect effect on comprehension. They contribute directly because discussions build understanding (Wilkinson and Son 2011). They contribute indirectly because the social aspect encourages students to select and read more books. As students read more, their fluency grows, thus freeing them to pay more attention to comprehension. Book club members need to read books that match their reading level. From among those books, they are free to select whatever title they want to read and discuss. The students in a book club can all read the same book. The book club could focus on a particular author—Patricia Polacco and Jack Gantos are just two authors who write for a number of reading levels—with each club member reading a different book by that author. Another approach is to find books at a number of reading levels on a particular theme (Block et al. 2009).

Book clubs include the four related activities (on page 106) that might be spread out over several days. Much of the time is spent reading, reflecting, and writing. Only then do the book club members come together to share and discuss.

Figure 5.3.   Reading Conference Record

Student Name _____   Date of Conference _____

Title of book student is reading _____

What page are you currently reading? _____ How much have you read since _____?

_____ pages

Part A: Interest and Motivation

• Is this book right for you? Do you find it interesting? What problems have you had reading it?

Part B: Comprehension

• What is the book about? What is the main character up to? Did you make any connections between the book and other books, between the book and your life? Have any questions come up while you were reading?

Part C: Goal Setting

• When do you plan to finish? What do you want to read next? Can I make some suggestions?

1. Reading a self-selected book for 10 to 20 minutes.

2. Writing a teacher-assigned journal response to the book.

3. Discussing the book with the other members of the club and sharing portions of the written response. This meeting is student-led; the goal is for students to learn how to discuss a book in depth.

4. Participating in teacher-led whole-class shares. If sharing takes place before the students begin reading, you build background knowledge and teach strategies such as story structure or summarizing. After the text is read, students share their responses to their book, discuss parts that were confusing, and recommend, or not, the book to others.

Structuring Independent Reading with Literature Circles

In a literature circle, a small group of students have a meaningful discussion of the same student-selected book (Daniels 1996). You provide three or four books (ideally related to the current unit) in which the students have expressed interest, and the students choose the one that appeals to the majority. You assign students roles that hold them responsible for certain aspects of the book or certain comprehension skills. (The roles change each time the group meets, so it's very important to model and practice each several times before letting the students fly on their own.)

Here's a step-by-step approach for getting literature circles up and running:

1. You introduce and model each of the roles, as originally developed by Harvey Daniels (1996):

   • The discussion director/questioner leads the discussion and asks questions.

   • The text connector makes connections between the text being read and previously read texts.

   • The vocabulary enricher discusses new and unclear words and phrases.

   • The literary luminary identifies passages that are funny, interesting, difficult to understand, or exciting.

   • The summarizer summarizes what has been read.

2. The students in each group select their book and determine how much of the text they will read before they meet for the discussion. They also select a role for the first book club meeting.

3. The students read a chapter or more of the text independently, develop the responses they will share during the discussion, and record these responses on their role sheet (for copies of these role sheets, see Daniels 1996). The discussion director develops questions, the vocabulary enricher lists words she found, the literary luminary marks book passages and makes evaluative statements, and the summarizer writes a summary.

4. The group discusses the text. (Since the discussion director keeps the literature circle going, you may initially want to assign this role to a particularly strong verbal student.)

5. During the discussion, you act as a facilitator, not a participant. But do help the students complete their roles. For example, if the vocabulary enricher has missed any new words, point them out; if the literary luminary failed to discuss a rich phrase, bring it to the group's attention.

6. At the end of the meeting, assign a new section for the students to read independently. Also assign each student a different role and distribute new role sheets to complete before the next meeting. (Once students are familiar with the roles and routines, they can do this on their own).

With younger and less competent readers it is best to begin literature circles using the role sheets. As the students develop reading ability and gain experience they can dispense with them. Research on literature circles indicates that the procedure improves students' general reading performance, their ability to discuss literature, and their motivation for reading (Davis et al. 2001).

The Second Road to Fluency: Teacher-Guided Practice

Small-Group Work

For some students independent reading is not enough to build fluency. Teachers need to create specific small-group and independent activities. Mrs. Rodriguez, a second-grade teacher, helps students with oral reading fluency during her small-group instruction. Today she is meeting with her below-grade-level reading group, most of whom are reading on a first-grade level. The class is studying wild animals and pets. Mrs. Rodriguez knows that this group cannot read the core anthology selections for this unit, so she finds a text at their reading level that deals with this same theme: *Harley, the Busy Dog*. The students echo-read the story, read it chorally, and whisper-read the story to build their fluency. Mrs. Rodriguez notices that Davasia has miscued on the high-frequency words *where*, *could*, and *just*. While the other students continue their whisper reading, she asks Davasia to reread the passage containing these miscues aloud and encourages her to work on her expression. Davasia reads the words correctly the second and third time, and Mrs. Rodriguez praises her.

In other group work Mrs. Rodriguez explains some of the guidelines for fluent reading, stressing when to pause, stop, and use punctuation and how to read with expression and intonation. She models fluent reading and encourages students to echo her back. When a student reads a passage with weak fluency, Mrs. Rodriguez encourages him to reread and improve his rate, accuracy, and expression. If these informal moves are used regularly, students' fluency will improve (Kuhn and Stahl 2003).

Independent Fluency Practice

For her students' independent work, Mrs. Rodriguez finds books that interest her students, uses some of them in small reading groups throughout the week, places leveled readers in book baskets at the students' tables for rereading, and creates fluency activities in the classroom fluency center. She models and practices these activities with small groups before including them in the center. Students are enthusiastic about these fluency practice activities and recognize that they are becoming better readers. With this increased confidence, they tackle longer and harder trade books.

REPEATED READINGS. The most well-known practice activity is the method of repeated readings (Samuels 1979). All other fluency development activities are derivatives of this basic idea. Mrs. Rodriguez introduces it to her below-grade-level group by following these steps:

1. She selects a short text from their current leveled book (one hundred to two hundred words) and explains the purpose of repeated readings.
2. She models fluent reading.
3. Each student reads the passage while Mrs. Rodriguez times the reading. She records the results on a graph.
4. The students read the same passage several more times during their independent time throughout the week. Each time they try to read it more smoothly, a bit faster, with fewer errors.

5. When individual students feel ready they read the passage again for Mrs. Rodriguez, who records the new reading and accuracy rates on the chart. This process is repeated until each student achieves the goal of eighty-five to one hundred words correct per minute. (See www.readnaturally.com/pdf/oralreadingfluency.pdf for suggested fluency rates.) Mrs. Rodriguez and the student study the graph together and discuss the student's success. It is important for students to attribute their success to their own efforts as this builds self-esteem and motivation.

6. Mrs. Rodriguez then repeats the process with a new passage. The proof is in the pudding. If a student reads the new passage at a quicker rate, she and Mrs. Rodriguez know automaticity is occurring: the student is applying what has been learned.

RED-HOT READS (Waite 2005). Mrs. Rodriguez includes this activity in the fluency center. She retypes a text students have previously read, *Harley, the Busy Dog*. At the end of each line she includes the number of words so that students can easily see how many words are in the line (see Figure 5.4). With this text is a green crayon, a yellow crayon, and a red crayon (you can also use markers) and a one-minute sand timer. Working in pairs, one student times the other's one-minute reading and monitors its accuracy, highlighting the last word read with the green crayon. Then the pair switch roles and time and record another first reading. They each do a second and third reading in the same way, using a yellow crayon for the second and a red crayon for the third. The goal is to increase the number of words read each time and become a red-hot reader. The students record the results of the three readings on a chart and demonstrate their improved skill during the next day's small-group meeting.

Figure 5.4. Retyped Story for Red-Hot Reads

Harley the Busy Dog	
Harley is a very busy dog. On Mondays he spends his	11
mornings over at the Hudsons playing with Meg and Kelly.	21
On Tuesday he gets to sleep in. But in the afternoon he	33
helps Sarah and her mother walk their new baby Owen.	43
Harley's days were so full with visits and walks that he	55
just could not keep up with his life. Until one day he	68
found an old Blackberry cell phone and brought it home.	78

BASKETS OF LEVELED READERS.   Mrs. Rodriguez promotes cooperative learning, so her students' desks are grouped in pods rather than lined up in rows. Each pod includes bins filled with leveled readers that match the group's reading abilities and support the themes students are currently studying. Some of the books have been read before; others are new. Students read (or reread) the texts, either independently or with a partner (their choice), at the following times:

- When they first enter the classroom in the morning.
- After they have completed their independent work.
- When the class is getting ready to go to lunch.
- After they have come back from lunch.
- Before recess.
- A few minutes before dismissal.

Mrs. Rodriguez watches and listens as the students read, checks their accuracy and fluency, and provides support. After they have followed this routine for a time, her students' fluency greatly increases.

Fluency-Oriented Reading Instruction

Steven Stahl and Kathleen Heubach (2005) have combined all the instructional techniques described in this chapter into a comprehensive approach to building fluency and reading ability that they call *fluency-oriented reading instruction* (FORI). FORI lessons always focus on reading comprehension. Students read material at their instructional level and are supported through repeated readings, partner reading, and independent reading. They are expected to read widely at school and at home. Many activities take place during a typical week of instruction:

- *Monday.* The teacher discusses the attributes of fluent reading and uses the first pages of the week's anthology selection to model them as the students echo back. She then finishes reading the story. Students who need additional help are pulled aside for more echo reading.
- *Tuesday.* The teacher uses the same story to develop comprehension by teaching the skills and strategies suggested in the teacher's manual. The students take the story home and read it to a family member.

- *Wednesday and Thursday.* Students select a portion of the story and reread it with a partner, trying to improve their fluency. Students also select books from the classroom library to read independently. They complete journal responses about the books and stories they are reading.

- *Every day.* Students are expected to take the main anthology story or their leveled books and independent reading books home. Parents are shown how to provide time for students to read at home and how to respond to and correct their children's reading. At the end of the week the students share their journal responses to the books and stories they have read during the week.

- *Every day.* Students should read independently every day. They may select books from the classroom or school library. The teacher meets with each student weekly to check progress, evaluate comprehension, and suggest new books.

Building fluency through repeated practice is important. Building fluency through independent reading is vital. We cannot judge ourselves a success if students learn to read but elect not to do so during the course of their lives.

Extending Your Learning

- Talk with your colleagues about what your school is doing to promote independent reading and fluency.

- Share what you know about children's literature with your colleagues. Have a virtual book exchange; share the most exciting new books you have read. Bring these books to your meetings.

- Type up text for red-hot reads and read-for-speed center activities. Share the texts with your colleagues.

- Brainstorm ways to help students choose appropriate independent books in the reading area/library.

- Find a teacher in your building or district who is great at running literature circles and arrange for her or him to model in your classroom.

Further Reading

• •

Blevins, Wiley. 2002. *Building Fluency: Lessons and Strategies for Reading Success.* New York: Scholastic.

Rasinski, Timothy. 2010. *The Fluent Reader: Oral and Silent Reading Strategies for Building Fluency, Word Recognition, and Comprehension.* 2d ed. New York: Scholastic.

What Does the Research Say About the Development and Teaching of Reading Comprehension?

As we know from our teaching, reading comprehension can be baffling. All the children in a group may be able to read the words in a story accurately and fluently, yet ask them to summarize the story or answer a few comprehension questions and vast differences appear. Some fourth graders can construct an elegant summary; others can report only one salient detail. Some students can answer literal questions, but ask them an inferential question probing why something happened and they are stumped. To help all students comprehend, we need to understand this complex mental process.

How Do Readers Comprehend?

Reading comprehension involves almost all the faculties of the human mind. To one expert, reading comprehension is "thinking guided by print" (Perfetti 1985); to others it is building bridges between the known and the new (Pearson and Johnson 1978). When we teach comprehension, we are teaching students to think. Because our tests and curriculums are so skills centered, many educators, even those who write about comprehension, have come to believe that comprehension consists of acquiring and using a set of skills or strategies. Yet, this is only part of the picture. Successful reading comprehension requires knowledge, motivation, metacognition, and strategies, each element contributing to the whole.

KNOWLEDGE. Comprehension begins with our linking ideas from one sentence to another. Our knowledge of grammar, vocabulary, and the world around us drives comprehension (Kintsch 1998). Consider the following paragraph:

> Early Monday morning Starbucks was crowded as people rushed in for their morning pick-me-up. People maneuvered and pushed for a place in line or jostled each other for the cream and sugar. Still waking up, John got in line, waited his turn, and ordered his latte. It was steaming

> hot. Three young men brushed by him. He momentarily lost his balance.
>
> Now there is a stain on his trousers.

Knowledge of vocabulary is necessary to understand *latte*, *steaming*, *stain*, and *trousers*. Knowledge of pronoun-noun relationships helps us understand that the coffee was hot, not the weather. An inference based on prior knowledge ties the last sentence in the paragraph to the ones before it. We infer that John spilled his coffee and that crowds at Starbucks had jostled him. Without knowledge, inferences, the glue of comprehension, are impossible (O'Reilly and McNamara 2007).

STRATEGIES. When the material being read is easy, knowledge construction drives the comprehension process. Strategies play an important role when the material is difficult—when we lack the necessary prior knowledge. Skills and strategies help us pay attention to what is important: to summarize what we have read, visualize important characters or settings, and make inferences and predictions or ask questions that keep us engaged. Some strategies help us determine the important ideas and others help us summarize them (Dole, Nokes, and Drits 2009).

METACOGNITION. Knowledge building and strategic thinking needs "minding": it requires metacognition. While part of our mind is constructing ideas and using strategies, another part is watching and evaluating the work. When things don't make sense, the watching-and-evaluating part sounds an alert and we reread; we try to recapture the sense we lost. Without metacognition we don't know or care when we construct gibberish in our head (Baker and Beall 2009).

MOTIVATION. Finally, comprehension requires motivation. The act of reading is not always easy. When understanding what we read is difficult, we have to push through. Even when reading is easy, we have to initiate the process, have a purpose, and see that purpose through. Some young readers can engage with a short picture book but are overwhelmed by a hundred-and-fifty-page novel; motivation is vital if they are to attempt it. Even on standardized tests, motivation is essential to work through the text passages and related questions (Guthrie, Wigfield, and VonSecker 2000).

Although comprehension involves all these factors, it is not easily reduced to a handful of skills. In fact, viewing comprehension as a set of skills may lead us astray. Comprehension is more complex than a list of skills found in a core program or set of state standards.

How Does Comprehension Ability Develop in Children?

The development of reading comprehension begins before children enter school, continues while they are learning to read, and is constantly refined throughout their lives.

The foundations of reading comprehension are built when David first begins to develop language (Lonigan et al. 2008). Slowly at first, then quickly, he builds the vocabulary (words and their meaning) necessary to understand the books he will later be reading. David is also figuring out grammar. This allows him to know in a given sentence who is the actor, what is the act, and what is the object and result: *John* (the actor) *hit* (the action) *the ball* (the object) *over the fence* (the result). Knowledge of grammar also enables David to understand how one sentence is linked to another through pronouns (*he, it*), conjunctions (*and, but*), and adjectives (*few, some*). By first grade David can understand books he cannot read, and the books he can read are well beneath his comprehension ability (Paris and Hamilton 2009).

Once in school David's comprehension is shaped by everyday language experiences and more formal instruction. Every subject in school builds David's knowledge and vocabulary, especially read-alouds. By most estimates vocabulary and prior knowledge are the most important ingredients in reading comprehension (Anderson and Freebody 1981; Davis 1944). Teachers foster comprehension by creating a curriculum that is focused on ideas and topics, not just strategies.

David learns that reading is different from engaging in a conversation or listening to a lecture. If we don't understand the person we are talking to, we can ask her to repeat or rephrase. While reading we can't query the author; we must repair meaning on our own. A lecturer will not stop to repeat a thought when we don't understand, but while reading we can stop and reread anytime we want. Speakers emphasize their ideas through intonation, inflection, and gestures. Writers, especially nonfiction writers, use print cues—headings, subheadings, and bold print—to convey emphasis. David must learn these signals (Willingham 2007).

When David is reading about a subject he does not know well, comprehension strategies help him over the bumps in the road. His teachers aid his development by teaching and modeling specific skills and strategies. He learns to read between the lines, make inferences, focus on the important idea, get to the gist, summarize, evaluate what he has read, and think critically. David will use these skills if he believes doing so is important.

When studying insects, a personal passion, David is willing to complete graphic organizers and summarize what he's read. When asked to complete a workbook page on cause and effect, he does so halfheartedly because learning skills for the sake of skills is not motivating. Motivation drives David to think critically.

What Is the Difference Between a Comprehension Skill and a Comprehension Strategy?

When we think of a skillful basketball player, we conjure up Michael Jordan, who can execute the most difficult shot with ease. Everything seems effortless, requiring little thought; it flows. Skills are automatic, well-practiced activities or thoughts. But basketball also requires strategic thinking like one player's purposefully guarding another or a team's running a designed play to take advantage of another team's weakness.

The same is true of reading. Most of the time we make inferences, focus on what is important, and ask ourselves questions without having to think about it. This skillful way of thinking just flows. A strategy is a mental act performed with deliberate awareness. Deciding it would be useful to stop for a moment and summarize what has been read is a strategy at work.

What we teach might start out as strategies, but over time they become well learned and automatic skills (Afflerbach, Pearson, and Paris 2008). As strategies are used and refined, they require less effort and are used with less conscious thought; but readers can always be deliberate and think strategically if it helps. For example, when reading becomes confusing, good readers stop, reread, and try to paraphrase; these are deliberate strategic acts.

How Many Strategies Do Children Need to Be Taught?

Core reading programs contain lessons that require teachers to teach between fifteen and twenty-five reading skills/strategies in an academic year (Dewitz, Jones, and Leahy 2009). However, reading researchers (National Reading Panel 2000; RAND Reading Study Group 2002) have found support for far few strategies. They focus on the following:

- *Predicting*—using knowledge from the text and personal knowledge to infer what will happen.

- *Making inferences*—inferring the feelings, motives, and traits of characters; the causes of events of history; and the processes of science.

- *Determining importance*—identifying the main ideas in nonfiction, the themes in fiction and poetry.

- *Summarizing*—getting to the gist and putting it into your own words.

- *Questioning*—asking yourself questions while reading to stay engaged and promote inquiry.

- *Understanding text structure*—using your knowledge of text structure to navigate fiction and nonfiction.

- *Monitoring comprehension*—realizing that what you are reading does not make sense and undertaking some act like rereading to repair your understanding.

These strategies are not distinct. Predicting is an inference. So is finding the main idea: authors rarely state the main idea explicitly. Determining importance is an essential step in summarizing, and questioning is a good way to monitor comprehension.

Core reading programs offer a much more complex curriculum than the seven strategies listed above, for several reasons. First, they have to cover all the skills and strategies on state reading tests, so the skills and strategies proliferate. Second, one skill is often taught under several different labels. In reality there is no difference between making inferences, drawing conclusions, and making a generalization—they all demand the same kind of thinking. Many core programs take a broad skill like narrative structure and, dividing it up into smaller skills like setting, character, and plot, lead teachers to believe there is more to teach and learn than there actually is. Third, some core programs present fantasy and realism or fact and opinion as skills, but they are characteristics of genre. In any case, teaching too many skills clutters the curriculum and makes little sense to students or to teachers (Dewitz, Jones, and Leahy 2009).

How Should Skills/Strategies Be Taught?

The most widely accepted model of comprehension instruction is the gradual release of responsibility (Pearson and Gallagher 1983; Duke and Pearson 2002). The teacher begins by explaining and modeling a number of related comprehension strategies. The prevailing view is that strategies should not be taught one at a time but as a suite; readers never use just one strategy, but employ various strategies as they are needed (Reutzel, Smith, and Fawson 2005).

After strategies have been introduced comes a long period of guided practice during which students try out the strategies. This is the most important phase, because teachers can guide students' thinking while the students are reading. Guided practice should be conducted in the context of real literature or a unit of inquiry in science or social studies. Research documents that strategies are best learned when the students have a real goal, like learning about science or understanding a novel (Guthrie, Wigfield, and VonSecker 2000). Strategies then become tools to achieve that real goal. Never choose a text because it will help students learn a specific strategy; select a text because it is interesting and will build students' knowledge, then use strategies as needed. Strategy workbooks do not work to improve reading comprehension (Block et al. 2009).

We know of no research that advocates a particular scope and sequence for teaching comprehension strategies. People who create core readers must, of course, put the strategies in a sequence, but they appear to be following no particular logic (Dewitz, Jones, and Leahy 2009). Core reading program developers argue that they have created a spiral curriculum, but the evidence suggests that strategies are not reviewed often enough to help struggling readers (Dewitz, Jones, and Leahy 2009). There are a few "universal" strategies, like predicting, making inferences, questioning, summarizing, and monitoring, that should be introduced early in the year and used whenever applicable. Other strategies, like using narrative or expository structure or finding the main idea or theme, are unique to particular genres.

How Can Growth in Comprehension Be Assessed?

This is the most common question teachers pose and the most difficult to answer. To measure comprehension you must first determine your view or theory of comprehension. If you believe that comprehension involves understanding the literal meaning of a passage, making inferences, and critically evaluating what has been read, select an assessment that assesses all these outcomes in the context of rich authentic text. If you believe that comprehension is grasping the literal meaning of the sentences in a short passage, then a cloze or maze test is sufficient. The assessments you use during the school year must at least match the conception of comprehension in your state's reading test (Leslie and Caldwell 2009).

The next problem in assessing comprehension is that your data will always be limited (Taylor and Pearson 2005). No single assessment tool provides a complete and accurate view of any child's comprehension. If you use more than one type of assessment, your conclusions will be more valid. Compare how your students perform while answering questions during a discussion with how they perform when answering multiple-choice or written-response questions and then decide whether you would rate their comprehension as strong, average, or weak. Repeat this comparative evaluation every few weeks and see whether their performance improves. Finally, choose passages for assessment at students' instructional level and about which they have some prior knowledge. You want to make sure limited word recognition ability and lack of prior knowledge are not the cause of comprehension difficulties.

When you interpret the results of a comprehension test, you need to consider the reader, the text, and how the task influences comprehension. The reader brings to the act of comprehension knowledge, motivation, and strategies. If her knowledge is rudimentary, her comprehension will be impaired. If she is not motivated, she will not perform. If she is not a strategic reader, she will not puzzle out the meaning of a complex passage. The text also influences comprehension. One student may demonstrate excellent comprehension when reading about gymnastics and miserable comprehension when reading about the Louisiana Purchase. A well-organized passage is easier to comprehend than a dense, inconsiderate text. Select a test with passages that represent a variety of topics and complexity in order to smooth out the differences in students' prior knowledge and reading ability.

Finally, some readers demonstrate strong comprehension when asked to retell a story orally but poor comprehension when providing short constructed responses or answering multiple-choice questions. You need to determine how much students' writing skills or knowledge of test-taking strategies affects their comprehension. What does it mean that a student demonstrates excellent comprehension when discussing his reading in a conference but stumbles when working on his own? Questions like these test your interpretive skills!

CHAPTER 6

Boost Your Core
Reading Program's
Vocabulary Instruction

Recently Peter was working with four struggling second graders as he modeled a reading lesson for a group of second-grade teachers. Two of these students were English language learners; for the other two, English was their first language. Peter began the lesson by introducing four key words and their spelling patterns: *drum*, *fish*, *tall*, *jam*. He pronounced the words for the students without showing them in print and together they segmented the words into phonemes and discussed the spelling pattern in each word. They also discussed the meaning of each word, because the more students know about a word's meaning the more likely they will retain it. Students cannot retain nonsense.

Peter: Our first key word is *drum*. Everyone repeat the word *drum*.

Students: *Drum*.

Peter: Let's count the number of sounds in the word *drum* and hold up one finger for each sound in the word. [The students say /d/ /r/ /u/ /m/, holding up one more finger for each sound they say.] Very good, yes there are four sounds in the word *drum*. What is the first sound that you hear?

Raul: *D*.

Peter: Yes the word *drum* is spelled with a *d*, but what sound does the *d* make?

Raul: /d/

[Peter proceeds through the rest of the sounds and then writes the key word *drum* on the whiteboard and identifies the spelling pattern *um*.]

Peter: What is a drum? Marialla, do you know what to do with a drum? [Mariella shakes her head, so Peter make a drumming motion on the desk and all the students smile.]

After going through this process with the word *tall*, Peter asks Travis, "What does *tall* mean?" Tavis raises his hand high above his head. He cannot give the opposite of *tall*, but he may not understand the concept of *opposite*. None of the students know any of the possible meanings of *jam*, so Peter starts with jelly, which they know. The word *fish* is not a problem.

This lesson and the vocabulary challenges probably sound familiar. As good reading teachers understand, vocabulary affects all aspect of learning to read. Vocabulary knowledge is essential for comprehension, word recognition, phonemic awareness, and fluency. To know a word well means you know its spelling, its phonics, its grammatical functions, and its meaning. Without word knowledge students are decoding nonsense words, and researchers do not endorse working with nonsense words. If you know the *um* in *drum* and the *ble* in *table*, you can decode the word *rumble*. However, if *rumble* is not in your oral vocabulary, you can't tell if you have pronounced the word correctly: there is no shock of recognition. The more you know about a word the better you retain it. Try delivering a fluent reading of a page from a book on theoretical physics. The vocabulary will slow you down, trip you up, until fluency becomes impossible. Unfortunately this is the experience for many struggling readers.

> **THIS CHAPTER WILL HELP YOU:**
> - Incorporate best vocabulary practices into a core reading program.
> - Select and teach critical vocabulary words when your core program does not.
> - Augment the word-learning instructional strategies in your core reading program.
> - Teach vocabulary for retention.
> - Incorporate into your instruction activities that build word consciousness.

Another challenge teachers face is students coming to school with widely different vocabulary levels (Graves 2006; Hart and Risley 1995). Research shows that a kindergartner from an upper-middle-class, college-educated home might have a vocabulary three times as large as his counterpart from a poor family. Hart and Risley also document that the language conditions in the home that fostered these vocabulary levels are vastly different. In the upper-middle-class home, the parents talk more, the child hears more words, and the parents provide more support as the child builds his language. These conditions are often absent in a low-income home. Vocabulary learning is also a matter of the rich getting richer.

The more words students know, the easier it is to learn new words. Each word they know has connections to other words, much like the complex interconnections of the cords in a fishing net. The more connections students can make between a new word and their existing vocabulary the more easily they will learn and retain the new word. Extra care, attention, and diligence must be taken to build the vocabulary knowledge of all students, especially those from low-income families.

Vocabulary Instruction in Your Core Reading Program

Core reading programs address vocabulary instruction in several important ways, but these methods can be improved. The teacher's edition identifies a number of vocabulary words at the beginning of each week that are necessary to understand the selection in the student anthology and leveled readers. These words are typically introduced in a very short piece of prose. The accompanying lesson asks the teacher to define the word, give an example of its use, and extend the explanation by contrasting the word with similar words. During the week the teacher can follow up with workbook practice and review the word when the students read and discuss the leveled readers. The words are assessed at the end of the week.

Core program vocabulary lessons are not tailored to the needs of particular students. The developers have made assumptions about which words are important to understanding the readings, but they do not know the vocabulary of *your* students. So you want to ask, *Are these the words my students need to know? Are there other words I should teach? Are there words I can ignore because my students already know them?* You can also improve the core instruction by providing richer explanations of new words and more contextually sensitive definitions. Finally, you can reconsider the practice activities and design others that you find more useful and more thought provoking. This chapter includes many ideas for doing so.

Core reading programs also build vocabulary by presenting lessons on word-learning strategies—using the dictionary; using context clues; and using prefixes, suffixes, and word roots. These word-learning strategies and accompanying workbook activities are spread throughout the units and are often not sequenced for maximum effect. For example, using context clues to infer word meanings is an important strategy, but it must be introduced early in the school year and practiced often before students can use it independently. This kind of concentrated effort to build skill and knowledge is often lacking in core programs. Core lessons often hopscotch from one aspect of vocabulary to another. One week students are exploring multiple meanings, the next antonyms and synonyms, and then context clues.

What Research Says About Vocabulary Instruction

Vocabulary is vital for reading, writing, speaking, and thinking. Words are the tools and substance of thought. Learning these words is an enormous task; research suggests that by the eighth grade a student must have a vocabulary of forty thousand words (Nagy and Herman 1987). Core reading programs address the challenge of building a large vocabulary only in part, leaving the greatest part of learning vocabulary in the hands of the teacher and the individual student. Michael Graves (2006) outlines a four-pronged vocabulary program that should be at the core of every classroom:

- Provide frequent, varied, and extensive language experiences.
- Teach individual words.
- Teach word-learning strategies.
- Foster word consciousness.

FREQUENT, VARIED, AND EXTENSIVE LANGUAGE EXPERIENCES. Language experiences include engaging read-alouds, deep and exciting discussions, writing for real reasons, and above all reading extensively and widely. Researchers argue that elementary students must add three thousand words a year to their vocabulary (Nagy and Herman 1987). In a core reading program a teacher will directly teach three hundred to four hundred of those words. The students learn the rest as they read widely across genres, listen to well-crafted read-alouds, participate in stimulating discussions, and write. During discussions and read-alouds teachers can focus on words that the core program does not. As children read widely they encounter many new words. It is estimated that the best reader in the class will read forty times as many words in a school year as the weakest reader (Anderson, Wilson, and Fielding 1988). Because of this vastly different exposure to words, the good reader's vocabulary grows and the weaker reader's does not. As we discussed in Chapter 5, this is why incorporating independent reading into your classroom is so essential.

TEACHING INDIVIDUAL WORDS. Core reading programs do help you teach individual words but you can and should make decisions about these lessons. Research tells us that direct instruction in word meanings should be deep and rich (Beck, McKeown, and Kucan 2002). Students need a clear explanation, several examples, a discussion of the characteristics that underlie the word, and the opportunity to connect the new word to their existing knowledge and experience (Stahl and Murray 1998). Students then need at least ten meaningful exposures to a word to ensure they know it and can use it (Beck, McKeown, and Omanson 1987). If the core program doesn't include these research-based ideas, you can add them to your instruction.

TEACHING WORD-LEARNING STRATEGIES.   The three main word-learning strategies are using context to infer word meanings; using prefixes, suffixes, and roots to determine word meanings; and using the dictionary to look them up. These important strategies should be taught early in the school year so students can apply them and build their own word knowledge. Teaching about word parts, morphology, must be sequenced throughout the school year to deepen students' knowledge of words and build their ability to construct word meanings. Teach word-learning strategies well, be explicit in your instruction, and gradually release the responsibility for applying the strategies to the students.

FOSTERING WORD CONSCIOUSNESS.   Fostering word consciousness is a rather elusive phenomenon. We might think of word consciousness as the affective side of learning vocabulary. Words are the tools, the *stuff*, of our language and thought. Words are used to convey what we mean, but words can also be studied and enjoyed in their own right. When we play word games like Scrabble and Boggle, rhyme words, speak in Pig Latin, question the origin of words, or marvel at the thousands of idioms in our language, words become a topic, not a tool. When students develop word consciousness, they know a lot about words and enjoy them. Many instructional activities develop word consciousness. When students collect their own vocabulary words in a personal dictionary, play with words, make up palindromes (*do geese see God*) or hink pinks (*What is a very tiny honey maker called? A wee bee*), or research word origins they are developing word consciousness.

Word-Learning Tasks

All word-learning tasks are not the same, and they differ by how much students already know about specific words, how much knowledge you want them to gain, and what the students are expected to do with the words. Some words are easy to teach because students have been using them for years in their oral language (*run, look, go*), while other words require brand-new conceptual understanding (*impeach, factor*). Many words represent new labels for known concepts (*bewildered* for *confused*). Using a word while writing a story requires more knowledge than matching a new word to its definition or filling in a blank on an end-of-the-week vocabulary quiz.

Vocabulary words can be sorted into groups called *tiers* (Beck, McKeown, and Kucan 2002). Tier one words are basic words found in everyday language—*sad, chair, girl.* These words very rarely need further instruction in school, since most students enter kindergarten with these words in their oral vocabulary and merely need to learn to pronounce them. Tier three words are specific to each content or domain—words like *infusion, ratify,* and *amniotic.* These low-frequency words must be taught when needed in a particular content area such as social studies, mathematics, or science. Tier two comprises words whose concepts are familiar to students, but the words themselves may be unknown—*disease, scolded, cacophony.* Instruction in these words will increase an individual's language ability, but tier two involves a huge set of words and teaching them requires many decisions. Five word-learning tasks suggested by Michael Graves (2006) help us better understand the nuances of vocabulary instruction.

Understanding Basic Vocabulary Words

Students come to school with varying oral vocabularies. While some children possess a substantial oral vocabulary of up to five thousand words, that of others is much smaller. Many students in the latter group are English language learners who do not use these words when they speak or understand them when they listen. It is of the greatest importance that students with weak oral language backgrounds receive explicit instruction in basic high-frequency words. The most commonly recommended list is *A General Service List of English Words* (West 1953). You can find this list at http://jbauman.com/aboutgsl.html. Read-alouds, the morning message, and rich discussions (see Chapter 3) are critical to learning these words.

Reading Known Vocabulary Words

Beginning readers have the huge undertaking of learning to read words that are currently in their oral vocabularies. Tier one words like *jump, swim,* and *surprise* are usually known by second grade. By the end of fourth grade, successful readers will have learned to read and write almost all the words in their oral vocabularies. However, this may not be true for ELLs and struggling students. They may still need reinforcement in words we assume they understand. Instruction in tier one words includes teaching high-frequency words and providing basic phonics instruction (see Chapter 4).

Understanding New Vocabulary Words with Known Concepts

Tier two words are unfamiliar words, but students often understand the concepts related to these words. A word is a label for a concept. Students may not know the words *tedious, imbibe*, and *ravenous*, but they are familiar with the concepts of boredom, drinking, and hunger. The word *ravenous* may be unfamiliar to many fourth graders, but they have all felt hunger pangs and understand what it means to devour their lunch. Again, ELLs may have great difficulty with this task, because they have difficulty matching the concept in their first language to the new English word.

Understanding New Vocabulary Words and New Concepts

The most difficult task is learning to read and understand tier three words—words that are rare, are unique, and represent new concepts. For example, with the words *photosynthesis*, *chlorophyll*, and *membrane* a teacher would need to build a great deal of knowledge about plants, their structures and processes, before students can understand the vocabulary words connected to these concepts. He could also build these concepts by conducting observations and simple experiments, sharing several simple texts through read-alouds, or have students read.

Clarifying and Extending the Meaning of Known Vocabulary Words

The final word-learning task is to clarify words with similar denotations and different connotations. A shed and a cabin are both small wooden structures, but one is more desirable for camping. For example, one student we know confused the words *thin* and *narrow* and thus writes, *Ms. Smith is very narrow*. Ms. Smith was not pleased. We can clarify and extend meaning by repeatedly exposing our students to known but similar vocabulary words in many contexts and carefully discussing the differences. Creating a semantic gradient is a powerful way to clarify word meanings. For example, students might arrange words like *warm, tepid, hot, cool, cold, freezing*, and *boiling* into a hierarchy to better grasp degrees of temperature (see Figure 6.1).

Third-grade teacher Mr. Avery starts the discussion by writing the word *freezing* on the left side of a chart headed by a series of words related to temperature and the word *boiling* on the far right side. He then asks, "Who can find a word that means a bit warmer than

Figure 6.1.   An Incomplete Semantic Gradient

warm	tepid	hot	cool	cold	freezing	boiling
freezing						boiling

freezing, but not boiling?" A student suggests the word *cold*. The discussion continues until all the words are sequenced.

Selecting Words to Teach

The developer of your core program will have selected between eight and twelve words for you to teach before the students read the selection. These lists may need to be modified. A lesson with too many known vocabulary words may be inappropriately easy for students who need more of a challenge. A lesson may also ignore words your students *do* need to know. When planning a read-aloud or working with text outside the core reader, deciding which words to teach can be quite daunting. Here are some guidelines:

- Choose words that are essential to understanding the text.

- Choose words whose meanings cannot be figured out from the context.

- Leave some words for students to figure out on their own by applying context clues and structural analysis. ELLs may not be able to use these strategies, so they may need these words taught explicitly.

- Choose words that are useful outside the text being taught. For example, in *Swimmy*, by Leo Lionni (1969), Swimmy the fish encounters many sea creatures as he explores the ocean floor. *Creature* is an excellent tier two word for instruction. It extends word knowledge and students will encounter it again in *Ranger Rick* magazines or their science reading.

- If the selection contains few valuable words, choose related words. For example the second-grade story *Mr. Putter and Tabby Pour the Tea*, by Cynthia Rylant, has only a few challenging vocabulary words—*wonderful*, *company*, *delight*, *share*, and *enjoy*. Build on these concepts by also teaching the words *fantastic*, *companion*, and *enthralled*.

- Choose words that you can explain to students in familiar and understandable terms.

- Avoid teaching tier one words such as *can*, *help*, or *chair* unless you have ELLs and then work with one or two small groups, giving brief examples reinforced by pictures.

Working with Core Vocabulary Words

The following lesson illustrates how to modify a core vocabulary lesson.

This week Mr. Avery's third graders are reading *Balto, the Dog Who Saved Nome*, by Margaret Davidson (1996), a core reader story about a sled dog team that rushed medicine for diphtheria to Nome, Alaska, and started the tradition of the Iditarod dogsled race. The teacher's manual's identifies only six vocabulary words for this selection: *telegraph, drifts, temperature, guided, trail*, and *splinters*. Mr. Avery realizes this is insufficient and adds *operator, disease, diphtheria, hitched, tame, alive, drown, traveling, nightmare*, and *limped*, for a total of sixteen words. By adding words week after week you can expose your students to approximately 550 new words in a school year as opposed to the 300 or so words the core reader prescribes.

Teaching sixteen words a week may seem daunting, but if we classify the words by word-learning task the challenge is less imposing (see Figure 6.2; note that none of the words are basic sight words). Two of the selected words are known words, *traveling* and *nightmare*, and the majority of the words stand for known concepts. So teaching words like *guided, trail, disease*, and *hitched* takes little time and minimal explanation. *Diphtheria*, a new concept, is the main problem in the story, so it is helpful for students to understand exactly how bad the disease used to be. Symptoms of diphtheria are somewhat similar to those of influenza; students know what the flu is and can use this prior knowledge to make connections. *Telegraph* also

Figure 6.2.   Vocabulary Words Classified by Word-Learning Tasks

Reading Known Words	New Vocabulary for Known Concepts	New Concepts	Clarifying and Extending Word Meanings
traveling	guided	telegraph	operator
nightmare	trail	diphtheria	temperature
	splinters	drifts	
	disease		
	hitched		
	alive		
	drown		
	limped		
	tame		

requires considerable explanation, because that means of communication is no longer used in our country. *Drifts*, as in snowdrifts, is a new concept in much of Arizona and Hawaii. Finally, *operator* and *temperature* require clarification. *Temperature* can refer to either climate or bodily temperature, and *operator* must be connected to how a telegraph is used.

Teaching Individual Words

Learning an individual word involves developing both a conceptual and contextual understanding of the word. Conceptual understanding is developed by exploring the characteristics that underlie a word and providing examples of its use. For instance, characteristics of the word *reluctant* include *being unwilling to do something, disliking something but having to do it*, and *struggling to reconcile what you should do with the difficulty of doing it*. Examples of its use might be telling a hard truth to a friend or confronting a difficult problem at work. Contextual understanding can be gleaned from how the word is used in the passage in which it appears: *Mrs. Jones was reluctant to talk to Bob's parents, her close friends, about his recent behavior problems in school.* Isabel Beck and her colleagues (2002) believe that vocabulary should be taught in a robust way that includes these characteristics:

1. Introduce the word by providing both a student-friendly definition using everyday language and an example of its use in a meaningful context. Provide a picture if it will help students understand the meaning. This obviously works best for nouns or verbs.

    a. Identify a class for the word:

- A hero is usually person, sometimes an animal.
- A pitcher is a container.

    b. Describe characteristics that underlie the word:

- When you are a hero you do something dangerous or scary that helps another person.
- A pitcher is a container that has a handle and a spout and that is used for pouring liquids.

2. Give examples and ask students for examples and nonexamples.

    a. Is Superman a hero? Can someone in the army be a hero? Could a school teacher be a hero?

    b. Can you think of someone who is brave? Can you think of a person who is not brave?

3. Have students use the word orally in a sentence, and provide corrective feedback as necessary.

Let's listen in as Mr. Avery teaches the words *tame* and *diphtheria* to his third graders. For many children *tame* is a known concept (they are familiar with cats and dogs even if they don't have pets of their own); however, *diphtheria* is most likely an unknown concept. Mr. Avery is teaching the words before the students read the story. He could also have defined *tame* while the students were reading, because the underlying concepts are known. However, *diphtheria* represents an unfamiliar concept that will impede his students' comprehension of the story if they haven't been introduced to it beforehand.

TEACHING WORDS WITH KNOWN CONCEPTS.   Mr. Avery places the following sentence on the board: *Many dogs that are part wolf never become tame. They never learn to trust people, or obey them either.*

Mr. Avery: If an animal is tame, it is not afraid of people. Wolves are wild animals and are afraid of people. When animals are afraid, they may attack whatever they are afraid of, including people. [Points to the word *tame*.] This word is *tame*. What is the word?

Students: *Tame.*

Mr. Avery: *Tame* is used to describe an animal. *Tame* means that an animal is not afraid of people and can usually be kept as a pet. Some tame animals can be trained to take orders from people. Let's look at the picture on our vocabulary card. It shows a person with a pet dog and cat. These animals are tame. Let's think of some examples and nonexamples of *tame*. Is a lion tame?

Students: No!

Mr. Avery: Think of some animals that are tame. Juan?

Juan: Is a wolf tame?

Students: No!

Mr. Avery: Kathy?

Kathy: I don't think that a bat is tame.

April: I agree.

Mr. Avery: What do you think, Jeffrey?

Jeffrey: Can a parrot be tame?

Students: Yes!

Mr. Avery: Let's practice using *tame* in a sentence. I'll go first: *After much training, the monkey became tame and loved being around people.* Think of a sentence using the word *tame*.

Saniyah: We adopted a dog from the SPCA and it was very tame.

Sarah: A black widow spider will never be tame.

Michael: The trainer's job was to teach wild animals to become tame.

The next day Mr. Avery has the students reexamine the word in the story. "Let's look back in the story about Balto and discuss how the word *tame* is used. The text says that many dogs that are part wolf never become tame. Balto was part wolf, so the fact that he was able to become tame and follow directions made him a very special dog."

TEACHING A NEW CONCEPT.   Teaching words that represent new concepts requires considerably more instruction and time. Let's listen in as Mr. Avery teaches the word *diphtheria*.

Mr. Avery: This word is *diphtheria*. What is the word?

Students: *Diphtheria*!

Mr. Avery: This is a difficult word, so let's first examine its pronunciation by breaking the word into syllables. Remember a word has as many syllables as it has vowel sounds. How many vowels are in the word?

Juan: I think there are four vowels in the word.

Mr. Avery [after quickly placing a check mark over each vowel]: Where do we divide the word into syllables? Remember we never divide diphthongs like *ph* and *th*. [With the students' help, he writes diph/the/ri/a on the board.] Everyone, say the word again. Diphtheria is a deadly infection or illness that spreads quickly. It mostly affects the nose and throat in children and older people. *Diphtheria* is not a word we hear often, because today the United States provides vaccinations or shots for children, so it isn't an issue here. Long ago, medication wasn't always available and many would die without it. In the Balto story, there is an outbreak of diphtheria, and many people may lose their lives if they do not receive the proper medicine. Think about a time when you had a really sore throat. Diphtheria is somewhat like that except, today, after a few days, you begin to get better with or without medicine. The unfortunate people in our story feel really sick too, but without the diphtheria medicine, they may die. Can you think of any very serious illnesses or diseases that we have today?

Sarah: Cancer. My aunt has cancer but she is getting better.

Michael: Parkinson's something-or-other. My grandfather has that and he takes a lot of medicine so he can walk.

Mr. Avery: That's right; those are very serious diseases.

Juan: Can people get diphtheria today?

Mr. Avery: None of you can, because when you were very little, not even one year old, you were given a shot, a vaccination, that prevents the disease.

Teaching for Retention

Vocabulary instruction does not stop with robust direct instruction but continues during the week to ensure that students remember the new words. Reading the words in context is just the beginning; now you must focus on retention. For students to retain the words you teach, they must use them regularly and frequently. Isabel Beck and her colleagues (1987) suggest that ten to fifteen exposures are necessary for students to own a word. Forms of exposure include reading the word, writing it in a meaningful context, thinking about its meaning, and comparing and classifying words. Core reading programs provide some practice with vocabulary words beyond the initial instruction. Students will read the words in their anthology and again in their leveled books. They can also complete some worksheets, the best of which compel students to think about and use the words in meaningful ways. But there is much more you can do.

Meaningful practice involves exploring the meaning of the word, comparing it to other words, and using it precisely. We can rank practice activities from superficial to deep. A word-find puzzle, which asks students to circle letters on a grid, is extremely superficial and promotes no thought about meaning or usage. However, if you ask, *Can a house perish? Why or why not?*, students are compelled to think about meaning. They have to decide whether an inanimate object can die and if so, does it do so literally or figuratively? When they express their justification in writing, they are using the word in a meaningful context. We suggest you design practice activities that will push your students to think about the meaning of new words.

Each week Mr. Avery evaluates the practice activities provided by the core program and designs some of his own. His students participate in some or all of the following activities to reinforce their knowledge of the words. Word learning must not be confined to a five-day lesson plan in which words are introduced on Monday and tested on Friday. Words should be studied, reviewed, and used throughout the year. Words learned the first week of school could be used with words learned the second and subsequent weeks. The five-day plan of the core reading program limits what the teacher and students can do to build vocabulary.

VOCABULARY NOTEBOOKS. Students keep a vocabulary journal (a simple spiral notebook divided into twenty-six sections, A through Z) in which they record the words they are taught and the words they discover in their own reading. With each word they record they include a definition, a sentence that shows how it is used, and a synonym or antonym if appropriate. They are encouraged to use this notebook when they write.

WORD ASSOCIATIONS. A series of questions ask students to match a word with a vocabulary word they have studied. This is not matching words with definitions but making meaningful connections between words to build a network of meaning. For example:

Which word goes with *injury*? (*limped*)

What word goes with *disease*? (*diphtheria*)

What word goes with *snow*? (*drifts*)

The students are not given the answers, as on a worksheet; they must generate their own responses.

SENTENCE COMPLETION. A common instructional technique is to ask students to write each word in a meaningful sentence, but often these sentences say little about their understanding of the word (e.g., *The animal is tame*). Beck and her colleagues suggest giving students sentence stems and having them complete the sentence and thus demonstrate the word's meaning.

The animal handler had to *tame* the lion so. . . .

The *nightmare* was so scary that I. . . .

I *limped* to the sidelines after. . . .

WORD CLASSIFICATION. Students take four words from their vocabulary list and classify them in some way—similar or related meaning, similar parts of speech, related to the same topic, or the same number of syllables. A useful graphic organizer for this activity is a simple two-column list in which the words are classified on the left, with an explanation for the classification on the right (see Figure 6.3).

Figure 6.3. A Word Classification

Words I Classified	Why They Are Classified
diphtheria *temperature* *disease* *breathing*	I put these words together because they are about the disease diphtheria in the story of Balto.

A variation is to have pairs of students challenge each other. The first student classifies the words and passes the graphic organizer to his partner, who must guess the reason they were classified.

SEMANTIC GRADIENTS. A semantic gradient is an organized list of words that help students explore degrees of meaning. It typically cannot be used with just one week's words; however, after students have collected vocabulary words over several weeks, they may be able to sort them by degree. For example, the words *pleased, joyous, bothered, perturbed, annoyed, happy, furious, angry, livid,* and *ecstatic* could be reorganized into a gradient from ecstatic to furious. Pair students and have the first partner construct the gradient. The partner's task is to make an adjustment if necessary. Figure 6.4 shows two semantic gradients, one in progress, the second refined. Students should discuss the words and their usage after completing the gradient.

Figure 6.4. In-Progress and Revised Semantic Gradient

In Progress	Revised
ecstatic	*ecstatic*
pleased	*joyous*
joyous	*happy*
happy	*pleased*
perturbed	*bothered*
livid	*perturbed*
bothered	*angry*
furious	*livid*
angry	*furious*

VOCABULARY IN WRITING.   During reading, word meanings are critical, but while writing students must also pay attention to proper usage. When we read *remembrance*, its root word makes the meaning clear, but uncertainty about usage results in sentence like, *She remembranced the afternoon picnic*. Writing gives students the opportunity to get the usage correct. Start with simple activities like having students complete sentences with the new vocabulary words from the core story. Then move up to having them use several words in a story.

"Probable passage" (Wood 1984) is a popular writing activity. First you introduce and explain the meaning of the new words. Then ask your students to help you organize the new words according to story elements: setting, characters, problem, and events. The example in Figure 6.5 uses words from the Balto story. After the words have been discussed and categorized, each student writes a story using the words. When they are finished, they read the Balto story and compare it with the story they created, discussing what they thought might happen and what happened in the published story. The probable passage technique is also an excellent strategy for developing prior knowledge.

It is important for students to use their new vocabulary words in their daily writing, and their personal dictionary is an essential tool. Students use it to find words for their journal responses, their short stories, and nonfiction writing assignments. Remind students to consult their dictionary and occasionally require them to use a specific number of new words in a journal response.

Word-Learning Strategies

The third prong of well-rounded vocabulary development is teaching word-learning strategies. Students need to use context to infer word meanings, use the dictionary to determine word meanings, and use word parts—prefixes, suffixes, and roots—to understand a

Figure 6.5.   Classifying Words for a Probable Passage

Setting	Characters	Problem	Events
drifts	Balto	diphtheria	guided
temperature	tame	nightmare	
		disease	
		limped	

word's possible meaning. Core reading programs teach all three strategies, but you should be cautious about the thoroughness and timing of the instruction. Often the strategies instruction suggested in core programs is far less thorough than the research calls for. For example, the context strategy in one current core program asks you to describe three types of context clues: definition/example clues, synonym/antonym clues, and general or prior knowledge clues. You model the strategy once, and then together you and the students use the strategy to determine the meaning of seven additional words.

Compare this with five-step approach recommended by Graves et al. (2011) for determining a word's meaning from context:

1. Read carefully and stop when you come to the unknown word.
2. Ask yourself, what is the paragraph generally about?
3. Read slowly from that point forward, looking for clues to the unknown word.
4. Go back and read the sentence or two prior to the unknown word.
5. Select a word or phrase that seems to capture the meaning of the term and try it out. If it doesn't make sense, try another word or phrase.

Graves (2006) cautions that learning to use context clues will take weeks, not days, of consistent work. Core programs may devote only a day or two to teaching context clues and then not review the strategy until several weeks or months have passed. Also, these important strategies should be introduced early in the school year so that students can use them successfully as they read throughout the year. The same caution should apply to other word-learning strategies. If your core program teaches dictionary uses only a few times during the year, alter the instructional emphasis. Teach the dictionary early and have the students use it often.

Activities That Foster Word Consciousness

Mr. Avery believes that vocabulary growth is stimulated when his students find words both interesting and exciting. Therefore he incorporates many word-consciousness activities throughout the week. These added lessons and asides provide the sparkle that may be lacking in the weekly routine of vocabulary instruction in a core program. An activity that spans the year—the wonderful word wall—keeps the students excited about words every day.

Early in the year Mr. Avery introduces the word wall idea. Each week the students are to search for new, interesting, and exciting words. On Monday the students share their words and post them on the class word wall (a chain of three-by-five-inch cards that by the middle of the year circles the walls of the room twice). The cards are color-coded, a separate color for nouns, verbs, adjectives, and adverbs. A word that can be used as more than one part of speech is posted on a separate card for each part of speech. When students present their new words they discuss the meaning, where they found the word, and use it orally in a sentence.

During the week, the word wall is used in a number of ways:

- Students are encouraged to add definitions and sentences to the word cards by attaching Post-its. Some cards have so many appendages hanging off them, they resemble porcupines.

- Students "walk" the wall with a partner and challenge each other to define various words. By midyear most students know all the words on the wall.

- Occasionally Mr. Avery has the students use the word wall in a practice activity. The word wall lends itself particularly well to the word classification activity described previously.

- The word wall is a natural source for practicing using the dictionary. By the middle of the year students often request more comprehensive dictionaries because they are unable to find words in the ones the school provides.

- The word wall spills over to the students' homes: parents report regular discussions about words and children searching dictionaries at slumber parties.

Throughout the year Mr. Avery tries to build his students' knowledge and delight in words. One week he may introduce a lesson on idioms and have his students collect idioms for the word wall. Another week students play words games like hink pinks (*What would you call an obese feline animal? A fat cat*). Another time he may focus on words with several meanings or stress the origin of a word. The following books provide activities for developing word consciousness:

- *Sparkle and Spin: A Book About Words*, by Ann and Paul Rand (Chronicle Books, 2006)

- *Word Wizard*, by Catherine Falwell (Clarion, 1998)

- *A Little Pigeon Toad*, by Fred Gwynne (Simon & Schuster, 1988)

- *A Circus of Words*, by Richard Lederer (Chicago Review Press, 2001)
- *Scranimals*, by Jack Prelutsky (Greenwillow, 2002)
- *Wordworks: Exploring Language Play*, by Bonnie von Hoff Johnson (Fulcrum Publishing, 1999)

Extending Your Learning

- Study the vocabulary instruction in your core reading program and think about what you learned the last time you taught these selections. Were there more words your students did not understand? Did your students still have questions about words or their usage after they were taught?
- With your grade-level colleagues, go through the teacher's manual and select vocabulary words to be taught for the reading selections. Keep in mind the needs of your students and whether these are tier two or tier three words.
- With your grade-level colleagues, examine the program's individual word instruction and decide how you might improve it. Could you find pictures to augment your teaching?
- Examine the program's word-learning strategies. Decide when in the school year they will be taught and how much you will need to augment the instruction provided.

Further Reading

We recommend consulting the following books to learn more about teaching individual words, teaching word-learning strategies, and helping your students become more conscious of words:

Beck, Isabel, Margaret McKeown, and Linda Kucan. 2002. *Bringing Words to Life*. New York: Guilford.

Graves, Michael. 2006. *The Vocabulary Book*. New York: Teachers College Press.

The article below takes these ideas into real classrooms:

Baumann, James, Donna Ware, and Elizabeth Edwards. 2007. "'Bumping into Spicy, Tasty Words That Catch Your Tongue': A Formative Experiment on Vocabulary Instruction." *The Reading Teacher* 62: 108–22.

CHAPTER 7

Build Knowledge
to Increase Understanding

Elmhurst Elementary School has recently completed its second round of benchmark tests to take the measure of students' strengths and weaknesses in reading and predict who is most likely to pass the end-of-year state reading tests. The five fourth-grade teachers want to focus on students' needs so they pore over the test results, hoping to discover data that will allow them to differentiate their instruction most effectively. Thirty-five percent of the fourth graders failed the tests (scored less than 70 percent). Not a promising result, since the state high-stakes reading test requires an 85 percent pass rate. The teachers know they have to focus on the 35 percent who failed, but how?

The benchmark reading test consisted of four passages: two realistic fiction narratives (one about a family lost in a snowstorm, the other about a girl trying to find a part-time job to earn money to buy birthday presents), a short biography of Benjamin Franklin, and a section on the praying mantis from an informational science text. The teachers examine the computerized results by skill area: finding the main idea, making inferences, using context clues, locating details, using the dictionary, summarizing, determining the author's purpose, and so forth. They discover that students had considerable difficulty making inferences, finding the main idea, and determining the author's purpose. Also, students were much more successful with the two narrative passages (answering more than 80 percent of the questions correctly) than they were with the Benjamin Franklin and praying mantis material (answering 50 percent and 58 percent of the questions correctly, respectively). This analysis highlights the skill deficit of the students but ignores the possibility that insufficient prior knowledge affected the students' ability to comprehend the informational passages. Knowledge may be more important than strategies for reading comprehension (Kintsch and Kintsch 2005).

The fourth-grade teachers decide to address their students' comprehension problems using skills workbooks their school district has recently purchased. They will continue their regular instruction from the core program three days a week. On the other two days they will teach comprehension skills and have the students practice these skills, reading short passages and answering the accompanying multiple-choice comprehension questions. The teachers will then discuss these exercises with their students and provide feedback, reteaching the skills as necessary.

At first glance this might seem an appropriate way to address the students' comprehension problems (and many schools make similar decisions), but if we look a bit deeper we see a significant flaw in this approach. When teachers "teach the test" they ignore equally important factors of reading comprehension because those factors are not assessed (Shepard 2010). Comprehension is much more than skills and strategies—*knowledge* drives comprehension. The more knowledge students have, the better they can employ strategies (O'Reilly and McNamara 2007). When comprehension tests, particularly interim benchmark tests, are examined item by item, we tend to forget about other important properties of comprehension—decoding, fluency, vocabulary, motivation and knowledge. Comprehension is a complex process, and the importance of knowledge is often overlooked. This chapter shows you some ways to enhance this aspect of reading in your core reading program.

THIS CHAPTER WILL HELP YOU:

- Understand that comprehension requires strategies *and* knowledge.
- Create extended lessons that build knowledge using texts from your core program and text you add.
- Activate students' existing knowledge when the core program does not.
- Build new knowledge needed for comprehension when the core program does not.

Knowledge and Comprehension Instruction in Your Core Reading Program

Core reading programs build students' knowledge by organizing the reading selections into units or themes and developing specific knowledge related to the selections before the students read them. Evaluations of core reading programs suggest that these attempts to build knowledge fall short of what many students need. The five or six reading selections in a typical core program unit are very loosely joined. The knowledge students gain from the first selection will not necessarily help them comprehend the subsequent selections. With few exceptions, the readings in core program units are grouped under vague titles that imply more than they deliver (Dewitz et al. 2010; Walsh 2003).

One typical core unit for the theme Our World starts with a humorous fiction selection about a teacher's jitters on the first day of school. All the leveled books are also tied to the idea of dealing with new experiences that cause anxiety. Unfortunately, this unified focus lasts for only one week. Next week, the selection is about a Korean-American boy receiving a letter from his grandmother and the pleasures of that correspondence. The third selection is a nonfiction piece about a suburban habitat shared by humans and wild animals. The fourth selection is also nonfiction, this time about penguins, and the last selection is about a child trying to find a pet her parents will approve. These five selections do not build common knowledge about the human condition or the animal kingdom. The title of the theme, Our World, is purposefully vague. (There is the infrequent unit in which all the fiction and nonfiction selections hang together—one built around a topic like the American Revolution or the development of communication—but that is the exception, not the rule.)

Every weekly core lesson begins by building knowledge in two ways. First, vocabulary instruction introduces new words and, in some cases, new concepts. The students read a two- or three-hundred-word passage on the same topic as the main reading selection and discuss the new words with their teachers, thus building knowledge. Second, teachers develop prior knowledge by following some guidelines in the teacher's edition for a specific knowledge-building lesson. The teacher asks questions and discusses concepts focusing on knowledge students need to understand the main selection. These questions assume students already have the knowledge and the teacher's job is to activate it, bring it to the forefront. This assumption is often mistaken: Many students need the teacher to *build* that knowledge.

What Research Says About Building Knowledge in Comprehension Instruction

The research on comprehension instruction is slowly shifting its emphasis away from teaching children to use strategies—finding the main idea, drawing conclusions, summarizing—and toward creating exciting units of inquiry in which strategies are used to learn a new idea and savor and delight in a new experience. Comprehension requires both strategy use and knowledge, and students with greater knowledge use strategies better (O'Reilly and McNamara 2007; Shapiro 2004). Knowledge guides the use of strategies. When readers perceive that things don't make sense, when prior knowledge is not helping them put ideas together, strategies help them over the rough spots. Knowledge makes everything easier. When students have a firm grasp of a topic it is easier to find the main ideas and summarize. Most inferences are impossible without knowledge, and knowledge enables students to ask better questions.

In studies on concept-oriented reading instruction (CORI), John Guthrie and his colleagues (2000, 2004) have demonstrated that students' comprehension skills and motivation improve the most when comprehension strategies are taught in the context of meaningful and engaging units of study. CORI (which focuses on science but whose principles apply to reading in the social sciences) focuses on three attributes—knowledge development, motivation, and strategy use—to produce engaged readers who have the cognitive or strategic skills necessary to understand what they read. These students are motivated, want to learn new ideas, are driven by interest and curiosity, and are socially interactive, collaborating to complete projects. Skills and strategies are tools, not goals. Teachers using a core program need to redesign the instruction so that knowledge development is a central focus.

Creating Units That Build Knowledge

Core reading programs include many excellent reading selections and can be the foundation for interesting and motivating extended lessons or units. You just need to expand on what the core program has begun. You might construct your own unit that lasts for two weeks. To begin your planning:

1. Read the selections in your core unit.
2. Decide which combination of fiction and nonfiction selections, read together, will build students' knowledge. A unit might be built around content like mammals or a theme like diversity and acceptance.
3. Look for fiction and nonfiction texts to supplement the core selections. Go beyond the books and make use of the Internet.

You can build extended lessons in a number of ways:

- *Around a topic.* Organize your core and supplemental nonfiction or fiction selections around a specific topic—lions, airplanes, computers.

- *Around a theme.* Select core and supplemental literature (short stories, novels, poetry) or nonfiction that exemplifies a dramatic or humorous theme—tricking an enemy, displaying courage in everyday life, living with pets.

- *Around genre/literary characteristics.* Select core and supplemental selections representative of a particular genre or literary characteristic—plot structure, suspense, or techniques for developing characters. A core program selection like *Officer Buckle and Gloria* (Rathmann 1995) could be the impetus for a unit studying ways of writing humor; add *Miss Nelson Is Missing* and *Miss Nelson Is Back* (Allard and Marshall 1985, 1986), about a teacher with clever ways to control her class; and conclude the unit with *First Day Jitters* (Danneberg 2000), about a teacher scared of her first day in a new school.

Some teachers worry about not teaching all the selections in a core reading program; they believe each selection is vital. But the thirty or so texts in the student anthology and the ninety-plus leveled books are the picks of editors, who could just as easily have picked other selections—and you can as well.

A Second-Grade Unit on Penguins

Ms. Katzman knows that the selections in her core program can become the basis of a unit or extended lessons that build her students' knowledge and stir their motivation. These units, which might last two or three weeks, do not follow the unit structure of the core program. Mrs. Katzman is leaving the structure of the core program but will return to it later.

Recent popular movies have made penguins a hot topic. Her core anthology includes *The Emperor's Egg*, by Martin Jenkins, a nonfiction text about how the emperor penguin lives and tends to its young. Ms. Katzman decides to use this text as the basis for a two-week unit in which her second graders study penguins in greater depth. They have been studying animal habitats in science, so studying how the penguin adapts to the extreme weather in Antarctica is a great tie-in. The text set she chooses, organized by reading level, is shown in Figure 7.1.

The goal of this unit is to study the lives of penguins and how they adapt to their environment. Since there are sixteen types of penguins living between the equator and Antarctica, students can choose a species to study and learn how the species has adapted to its environment. Students will demonstrate what they have learned about a specific type of penguin by creating a poster that includes pictures, a physical description, behavioral characteristics,

Figure 7.1. Text Set for a Two-Week Penguin Lesson

Core Anthology Selection	*The Emperor's Egg*, by Martin Jenkins
	"My Father's Feet"
Read-Aloud Selection	*Wow! It's Great Being a Duck*, by Joan Rankin
Core Leveled Books	*Antarctica's Challenge* (above grade level)
	Eggs (on grade level)
	Staying Warm (below grade level)
	Animal Babies That Hatch (ELLs)
Above-Grade-Level Enrichment Texts	*Mr. Popper's Penguins*, by Florence and Richard Atwater
	Penguins! by Gail Gibbons
	Penguins! (National Geographic Kids), by Anne Scheiber
	Penguins, by Emily Bone
	Penguins, by Bobbie Kalman
	Penguin (Life Story), by Claire Robinson
	A Tale of Antarctica, by Ulco Glimmerveen
	In Antarctica, by Marilyn Woolley
	The World of Penguins, by Jenny Markert
	My Penguin Osbert, by Elizabeth Kimmel
On-Grade-Level Enrichment Texts	*The Penguin, A Funny Bird* (Animal Close-Ups), by Beatrice Fontenel
	Tacky and the Emperor, by Helen Lester
	Penguin Pete, by Marcus Pfister
	Life Cycle of an Emperor Penguin, by Bobbie Kalman
	Playful Penguins! by Sally Grindley
	Summer in Antarctica, by James Talia
Below-Grade-Level Enrichment Texts	*Penguins Can Go!* by Teddy Jones
	The Penguins Are Going on Vacation, by Catherine Bittner
	Plenty of Penguins, by Sonia Black
	Clever Penguins, by Beverly Randell
	Antarctica, by Lucy Bowman

and a habitat description. They will present the poster to the class as they give a short oral report. The two-week lesson plan is shown in Figure 7.2; at times the students participate in guided reading; at other times, they work independently.

The core teacher's manual suggests that students preview the anthology story by taking a picture walk and then, working with the teacher, developing the first two columns of a K-W-L chart, listing what they know (K) and generating questions about what they want to learn (W). At the end of the unit they will list what they learned (L). Ms. Katzman likes the activity but wants to make it more engaging, so she has the students complete an anticipation guide on penguins (see Figure 7.3) to challenge their knowledge and extend their learning. This stirs up considerable debate and argument as students consider penguin types and roles. To resolve their conflicts, the students will have to read more than the core selections.

The unit project, posters, and reports on penguins provide a motivating and tangible goal. As students read, take notes, discuss, and think they are building the knowledge necessary to create their posters and develop their oral reports. They will also at the end of the unit take a second look at their anticipation guide and reconsider what they thought they knew. Finally, the unit provides the context and the reasons to employ comprehension strategies necessary for thinking.

A Third-Grade Historical Extended Lesson

This unit or extended lesson begins with a selection from the core program, *Amelia and Eleanor Go for a Ride* (Ryan 1999), which like most core selections is a picture book. The story is based on a relatively obscure event in the 1930s, the meeting and airplane flight of Amelia Earhart and Eleanor Roosevelt. Few students will have any related prior knowledge. In the picture book, pioneer aviator Amelia Earhart and first lady Eleanor Roosevelt have an adventure in a plane after eating dinner at the White House. (They did in fact fly together, but another pilot, not Amelia, was at the controls.) The teacher's manual encourages teachers to use a web to activate students' prior knowledge about the two ladies. The only response this warm-up activity may generate is blank stares.

Amelia Earhart and Eleanor Roosevelt are probably unknown to most third graders, and considerable knowledge needs to be built, including:

- The early history of aviation and the challenges of flying long distances.
- The special and rare role of female aviators in the early days of aviation.

Figure 7.2. Penguin Two-Week Lesson Plan

Week One	Monday	Tuesday	Wednesday	Thursday	Friday
Whole-Group Read-Alouds	*Penguins!* by Gail Gibbons	*Penguins!* by Gail Gibbons	*My Penguin Osbert*	*My Penguin Osbert*	Discuss and describe writing project
Small-Group Guided Reading	Begin anticipation guide Read leveled books and update anticipation guide	Discuss leveled books and update anticipation guide Generate new questions about penguins	Read an additional book on penguins and discuss in small groups Update anticipation guide	Discuss the next book and finish updating the anticipation guide Generate new questions about penguins	Introduce penguin life-cycle graphic organizer for next week
Independent Work	Students continue to read additional books on penguins; they search for additional information and complete their anticipation guides; they also work at fluency, word study, listening, and writing centers.				

Week Two	Monday	Tuesday	Wednesday	Thursday	Friday
Whole-Group Read-Aloud	*A Tale of Antarctica* Introduce writing/poster project	*Tacky and the Emperor*	*Tacky and the Emperor* Review progress on penguin posters	*Penguin*, by Claire Robinson	Students share their writing/poster projects
Small-Group Guided Reading	New text, selected by reading level Guided reading focusing on strategies from the core; low group still works on decoding and fluency Students develop questions	Reread Monday's text Guided reading focusing on strategies from the core and student-generated questions Low group still working on decoding and fluency	Select a second text by reading level Guided reading focusing on strategies from the core and student-generated questions Low group still working on decoding and fluency Review progress on the writing/poster project	Reread Wednesday's text Guided reading focusing on strategies from the core Review progress on the writing/poster project	Meet with low group to continue work on decoding and fluency
Independent Work	Students continue to read additional books on penguins; they develop information necessary to complete their penguin posters; they also work at fluency, word study, listening, and writing centers.				

Figure 7.3. Anticipation Guide for Emperor and Adelie Penguins

	Before Reading	Statement	After Reading	Where You Found the Information
1	Agree/Disagree	The male emperor penguin is the smallest penguin in the world.	Agree/Disagree	
2	Agree/Disagree	Adelie penguins feed mostly on Antarctic krill.	Agree/Disagree	
3	Agree/Disagree	The female emperor penguin leaves to get food while the male sits on the egg.	Agree/Disagree	
4	Agree/Disagree	The egg is sat on and kept warm for two months.	Agree/Disagree	
5	Agree/Disagree	Adelie penguins arrive at their breeding grounds in June or July.	Agree/Disagree	
6	Agree/Disagree	It takes a week for an emperor penguin egg to hatch.	Agree/Disagree	
7	Agree/Disagree	Adelie penguins make a nest out of stones.	Agree/Disagree	
8	Agree/Disagree	All penguins live in very cold water.	Agree/Disagree	

- A summary of the trying times of the 1930s, especially the harsh economic conditions.
- President Franklin D. Roosevelt, his programs, and his paralysis.
- Eleanor Roosevelt as first lady and her role as the eyes, ears, and feet of the President.

Ms. Stibbe, the new third-grade teacher, assembles the text set—including read-alouds, core program selections, core leveled books, and supplemental texts for literature circles—shown in Figure 7.4. She spends a significant portion of her whole-class time during the

Figure 7.4. Text Set for Extended Lesson on Amelia and Eleanor

Core Program Selections	*Amelia and Eleanor Go for a Ride*, by Pam Muñoz Ryan
	Wings of Hope, by Marianne J. Dyson
Leveled Books	*Meet Eleanor Roosevelt* (above grade level)
	Meet Amelia Earhart (on grade level)
	Amelia Earhart: An American Flying Pioneer (below grade level)
	Our Nation's Capital (ELLs)
Read-Alouds	*A Picture Book of Amelia Earhart*, by David Adler
	A Picture Book of Eleanor Roosevelt, by David Adler
Above-Grade-Level Enrichment Texts	*Amelia Earhart: This Broad Ocean*, by Sarah Stewart
	Our Eleanor: A Scrapbook of Eleanor Roosevelt's Remarkable Life, by Candace Fleming
On-Grade-Level Enrichment Texts	*Roosevelt: An Inspiring Life*, by Elizabeth MacLeod
	Eleanor Roosevelt: First Lady of the World, by the editors of *Time for Kids*
	Franklin D. Roosevelt: A Leader In Troubled Times, by the editors of *Time for Kids*
	They Led the Way: 14 American Women, by Johanna Johnston
	Tar Beach, by Patty Webb
	A Picture Book of Helen Keller, by David Adler
	Airplanes, by Darlene R. Stille
	High-Flying Airplanes, by Reagan Miller
Below-Grade-Level Enrichment Texts	*Who Was Amelia Earhart?* by Kate Boehm Jerome
	Eleanor Roosevelt and the Scary Basement, by Peter Merchant
	Amelia Earhart, by Philip Abraham
	Airplanes, by Gail Saunders-Smith

first few days building the students' knowledge. She starts with a timeline so students will know when the events took place. During the discussion she has the students place their relatives on the timeline so they can personally relate to the era. (See Figure 7.5.)

Next, Ms. Stibbe shows two short videos so students can see into the past. One is a sixteen-minute summary of Eleanor's life (www.youtube.com/watch?v=bTLL9dad2a4&

Figure 7.5.   Timeline for Amelia and Eleanor

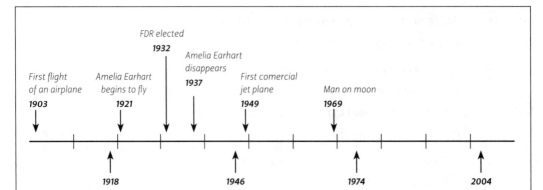

feature=related); the other documents the accomplishments of Amelia Earhart (www.youtube .com/watch?v=4COKAGaGN9U&feature=fvst). Having set the stage, Ms. Stibbe reads aloud *A Picture Book of Amelia Earhart* (Adler 1999) and *A Picture Book of Eleanor Roosevelt* (Adler 1995) to expand her students' knowledge. She uses the graphic organizer in Figure 7.6 to build parallel biographies as the students discuss the books and adds to it throughout the week as the students continue to learn about the lives of these two women. At the end of the week, students complete a Venn diagram comparing and contrasting the lives of the two women and their accomplishments. The goal is for the students to recognize and appreciate Amelia's and Eleanor's common courage.

During the second week, the unit expands beyond the core program selections in order to deepen the students' knowledge of Earhart, Roosevelt, and other famous women of the 1930s. The students read independently and participate in literature circles. They also create a newspaper article about a great woman in history. The article needs to contain a headline, important events, illustrations, and a fictitious interview with the woman about the great impact she had in American society. At the end of the week the students share what they wrote. All this time, Ms. Stibbe continues her differentiated small-group instruction on word recognition, fluency, and comprehension.

Figure 7.6.   Dual Biography Graphic Organizer

	Amelia Earhart	**Eleanor Roosevelt**
What were this person's major accomplishments?		
What were the important events in this person's life?		
Childhood		
Education		
Adulthood		
Death		
What can we learn from this person's life?		

Additional Decisions About Knowledge Development

When a teacher-created unit extends beyond the single week core programs typically allocate for reading one selection, important decisions need to be made. First, you must consider which core anthology selections will be pushed aside. A core selection rarely needs to be totally ignored: students can often read unrelated stories in the core program, as well as leveled books, independently. Second, when you turn a core selection into a two-week unit it is important to have a meaningful goal, a project. If students are excited about these projects from the beginning, they will plunge into their extra reading with greater interest and engagement. Third, it is important to keep the volume of reading high so students read much more than the core program suggests.

Techniques for Activating Prior Knowledge

Often children are assigned stories they already have the requisite knowledge to understand. This does not mean they will use that knowledge to make inferences or build connections between the text and their experiences. Researchers refer to this as *inert knowledge*. For example, take the stories *Bread and Jam for Francis* (Hoban 1995), about a very fussy eater, or *Ira Sleeps Over* (Waber 1975), about a boy's fear of a pending sleepover minus his favorite blanket. Most children have these experiences in their background, but this doesn't mean they will employ that knowledge to relate what they know to the text. Therefore, it's important to bring these experiences to the forefront. The strategies that follow help students activate knowledge they already have.

WEAVING STRATEGY.   This strategy, designed by Jane Hansen and P. David Pearson (1983), helps students apply what they know to the story they are about to read. First you pose a question that taps into the students' prior knowledge: *Have you ever moved to a new neighborhood? What was it like?* After some discussion the students write some of the responses on strips of gray construction paper (to simulate the brain's gray matter!). Then you pose a new question: *In this book a boy will move to a new neighborhood. How do you think he will make friends?* In essence you are asking the students to predict based on some information from the text. Write the predictions on the board, and have students copy them on strips of colored paper, which they then interweave with the gray strips, tangibly illustrating that readers must combine what they know with what the text says to comprehend the story.

K-W-L (Ogle 1986).   This is a venerable technique specifically designed to activate prior knowledge when reading informational text. Place the now very familiar chart (see Figure 7.7) on the board and begin a whole-group discussion. Note that this is the original K-W-L chart. Over the years, in numerous books and endless staff development sessions, the bottom two pieces were lost and neglected. We believe the neglected pieces are important—students must examine the texts they will be reading (Categories of Information We Expect to Use) and consider other sources of information (Where We Will Find Information).

You typically begin with a brainstorming session in which the children share what they know. If the information is incorrect, express some doubt and rephrase their statement as a question: *I'm not sure that is correct; let's make that one of our questions.* In the next part of the discussion, have students preview the texts they will be reading, looking at headings, subheadings, and graphics, and ask, *What information do you expect to use?* Previewing guides the students' inquiry and helps them understand how the text is structured. Next, let students generate questions (with your guidance) about what they want to learn. If they fail to ask some important questions, add them to the chart yourself. Next, have students discuss where else they will find the answers to their questions. After students have read and investigated, they will record what they have learned in the final column.

Figure 7.7. K-W-L Chart

What I Know (K)	What I Want to Know (W)	What I Learned (L)

Categories of Information We Expect to Use	Where We Will Find Information

PREREADING PLAN (PREP). The PreP strategy was developed by Judith Langer (1981) as a technique to activate and assess students' prior knowledge. You can use it to find out what students know, assess that knowledge, and then expand it. Begin by selecting one or more key words or concepts from the text and write them on the board. Then say, *Tell me anything that comes to mind when you hear the word [blank].* Write the students' ideas on the board and help them build a network of ideas: *What made you think of. . . ?* Give them the opportunity to weigh, reject, accept, and revise the ideas of others. Then ask, *Based on our discussion and before we read the text, have you any new ideas about [blank]?* PreP is more than brainstorming or listing ideas on a K-W-L chart; it is an attempt to formulate a coherent network of ideas. Through their discussion, students probe their memories and think more carefully about the topic.

A teacher at Elmhurst, Mrs. Barr, used the PreP approach to introduce a unit on the Civil War. When she asked students to tell her anything that came to mind about the Civil War she was flooded with information:

Mrs. Barr: You all know quite a bit, let's list some of your ideas on the board.

[She records the following ideas: *Lincoln, assassination, ironclads, slavery, North, South, Harriet Tubman, the underground railroad, the Gatling gun, freeing the slaves, Gettysburg.*] What made you think about Lincoln and his assassination?

Mark: Because the people in the South hated Lincoln and wanted to keep their slaves.

Mrs. Barr: So based on our discussion do you have any new ideas about the Civil War?

Juan: Was it mainly about slavery and setting them free?

Mrs. Barr: So that will be one of our goals, to find out why the war began.

Techniques for Building New Knowledge
• •

The creators of a core program do not know how much your students know. Often students lack the requisite knowledge for comprehending a text in a core anthology, especially non-fiction, so you must build that knowledge before they read. There are many techniques you can use: picture books, videos, the Internet, your own explanations.

PICTURE BOOKS.   One of the easiest means of building knowledge is to read a picture book that anticipates the conceptual knowledge students will need to understand the selection in the core program. You could prepare students for the story about an anxious teacher's first day of school, *First Day Jitters* (Danneberg 2000), by reading *Wemberly Worried* (Henkes 2000), the story of a mouse that worries about everything, and letting children explore their own fears and how to handle them. A nonfiction selection about astronomy could be introduced by reading *Planets*, by Gail Gibbons (2000). It may take some searching to find the right book: consult your school librarian or use the advance search function on Amazon.com.

VIDEOS.   Video is a neglected means for developing students' knowledge, and the Internet is a great resource. Start by searching www.youtube.com. Develop some prior knowledge before the students view the video, and set a very specific purpose for watching it. You can and should stop the video at various points to ask questions and clarify new ideas. Afterward review the purpose and discuss what the students learned. Add the knowledge gained from the video to a concept map (see below).

CONCEPT MAPS.   Reading a picture book or showing a video is probably not sufficient. The knowledge students gain must be developed and organized, and creating a concept map is an excellent way to do so. For example, if the selection is about whales you can introduce it with *A New True Book: Whales and Other Sea Mammals* (Posell 1982). After reading the text help the students develop a concept map about whales (see the example in Figure 7.8). Once the skeleton of the concept map is in place, the students can add to it as they learn new information.

Extending Your Learning

Building prior knowledge is an essential aspect of effective reading comprehension instruction. At times you can tinker with an individual core selection and build students' prior knowledge. Other times you may want to expand a basal selection into a two-week instructional unit. Try these activities with your colleagues:

1. Study a core program's reading selections and decide whether you will need to activate knowledge students already possess or build new knowledge. Discuss the best ways to build that knowledge.

Figure 7.8.   Concept Map for Whales

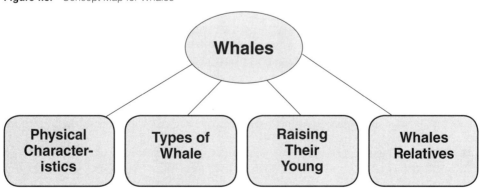

2. Read a few of the knowledge-building lessons in the teacher's manual and decide how you might go beyond them. Think about what students need to know in addition to vocabulary.

3. Pick one selection in the core anthology that can be expanded into a two-week lesson. Develop text sets and activities for these extended lessons.

Further Reading

Fisher, Douglas, and Nancy Frey. 2009. *Background Knowledge: The Missing Piece of Comprehension Instruction*. Portsmouth, NH: Heinemann.

Marzano, Robert. 2004. *Building Background Knowledge for Academic Achievement*. Alexandria, VA: Association for Curriculum Development and Supervision.

CHAPTER 8

Develop Comprehension
in Small Groups

Five third graders and their teacher, Mrs. Richman, are reading the story "My Father Never Takes Me Fishing," by Jane Kurtz:

> Three months ago, when Grandpa went on a fishing trip to Alaska, my dad said he would take me fishing.
>
> "Maybe Monday night when I get home," he said.
>
> But Monday night he had a meeting and didn't get home until late. By then I couldn't even care about fish.
>
> "Saturday, for sure," he said.
>
> But on Saturday our dog ate something rotten, and we had to take her to the vet.
>
> "Sunday a month from now, the twenty-first of June," he said.
>
> But when that day came, he forgot.
>
> And I forgot.
>
> "Other people's fathers take them fishing," I said. "Other people catch thousands of fish."
>
> "Don't get your hopes up," he said. "I'm not the world's greatest fisherman. I may be the worst."
>
> The next Tuesday night my dad and I played checkers.
>
> "Grandpa sent me a picture from Alaska," I said. "I'll show it to you at supper."
>
> "Speaking of supper," he said, "what would taste good?"
>
> "Fish," I said.

Dad pointed at the checker board. "Crown me," he said. "I think we have some fish sticks in the freezer."

"Grandpa says that fresh fish tastes better than fish sticks," I said.

"Crown me again," he said.

"Grandpa says, 'Give me a wild stream, some warm sun, and a fishing pole,'" I said. "Grandpa says that fishing makes your blood red and your eyes bright."

At this point Mrs. Richman asks the students to summarize the story:

Mrs. Richman: What is the story about? What has the author told us?

Roberto: A boy wants to go fishing but his father won't take him.

Mrs. Richman: Can anybody add to what Roberto told us?

Julia: He has a mean dad.

Mrs. Richman: Do you all agree that the dad is mean? What did the author tell us that gave you that idea?

Dajuan: 'Cause he keeps saying he will take him fishing, but they never go.

Mrs. Richman: Does the author tell us why the dad doesn't take the boy fishing? Does he give us any information? [There are no responses.] What happens the first time? Why didn't they go fishing?

Emma: 'Cause Dad was late.

Mrs. Richman: I have another question. Why does the boy, and are you sure it is a boy, keep talking about Grandpa? Why is he important to the story?

Emma: I think that the grandpa is nice and he takes the boy on trips, but the dad will not.

Mrs. Richman: If that is so, what is the boy trying to do? What is the boy's goal?

Roberto: He wants to go fishing like his grandpa.

Mrs. Richman: Why did the author have the boy keep talking about the grandpa? How does the grandfather help the boy get to his goal? [There are no responses.]

These five average readers are beginning to be able to summarize the story. They understand the characters and their goals, but it is difficult for them to get deeper into the motives of the characters. They don't like the dad, because he doesn't grant his son's wish, and they cannot enter into the mind of the boy and see that he is using the example of the grandfather to cajole the father. This is not an easy inference, but it is essential to fully understanding the story.

Small-group guided comprehension is essential to develop students' thinking. Through these discussions you model and mold your students' thinking. In guided comprehension you bring knowledge and strategies together as you show students how to comprehend the text—help them understand stories, poems, and articles. You show them how to connect one idea to another, when to use a strategy like predicting or summarizing, and when to link what they are reading to their prior knowledge. Guided comprehension is coaching: getting students ready for their independent reading and helping them solve problems presented by increasingly complex text.

Small-Group Comprehension Instruction in Your Core Reading Program

The teacher's edition of core programs provides directions for before-, during-, and after-reading activities. Before-reading instruction includes teaching vocabulary, developing prior/new knowledge. As noted in Chapters 6 and 7, these lessons can be modified so you build the knowledge and teach the vocabulary your students need. Next, most core programs suggest previewing the selection, predicting what it will be about or what will happen, and then setting a purpose for reading. These activities should not become a ritual, but you can draw on them as needed. Ultimately the students, not the teacher, should set the purpose for reading.

> THIS CHAPTER WILL HELP YOU:
> - Select texts from the core program and beyond for a guided comprehension lesson.
> - Examine a reading selection and identify ways to help readers overcome comprehension problems.
> - Promote comprehension through guided reading.
> - Differentiate comprehension instruction for all types of students.

The teacher's edition provides a wide range of page-by-page questions for every story in the student anthology; 70 percent of what teachers are directed to do while the students are reading involves asking questions (Dewitz, Jones, and Leahy 2009). Some of these questions are valuable, some are not, and there are more questions than you need. Questions focused on decoding, structural analysis, and grammar are distractions when the primary goal is comprehension (McKeown, Beck, and Blake 2009). Most core programs suggest that teachers—but not students—think aloud and model strategies, and students and teachers fill in graphic organizers. There are also suggestions for dealing with English language learners, teaching other comprehension strategies, making connections with other content areas, and presenting very brief lessons on grammar and literary devices. Bottom line, there is more to do than can or needs to be done, so making instructional decisions is critical.

What Research Says About Small-Group Comprehension Instruction

Researchers have consistently affirmed the value of small-group guided reading instruction for building comprehension (Taylor et al. 2000). When Rosenshine and Meister (1994) compared the value of explicit instruction in comprehension strategies with teacher-guided discussions, they found that small-group discussions were more valuable. Indeed, successful comprehension instructional approaches like using transactional strategies (Brown et al. 1996) and reciprocal teaching (Palincsar and Brown 1984) rely almost exclusively on small-group guided discussions. Instructing students while they are reading provides the best opportunity to promote the type of thinking that will foster understanding. During reading, you can help students make connections among ideas in the text, draw inferences, relate the text to prior knowledge, and repair understanding if comprehension breaks down.

Research also suggests that a guided comprehension lesson should focus on the ideas in the text, not strategies (McKeown, Beck, and Blake 2009). You need to help students understand what the selection is about, put ideas together, and solve problems the author created. Stopping to ask students to visualize a scene or make a prediction is necessary only when doing so helps students understand the text.

After students have finished reading, they can consolidate their understanding by summarizing what they have read; creating a graphic organizer; expressing their ideas through drama, music, or art; answering questions that demand higher-level thinking. We also recommend reading the text a second time (a practice rare in most programs), focusing on difficult parts and considering the author's craft (figurative language, unique plotting devices, etc.).

Planning Your Guided Comprehension Lessons

Mrs. Richman plans her comprehension lessons carefully; she rarely wings it. (And neither should you!). Her planning includes selecting the texts, studying the lessons in the core reading program, and when necessary modifying the lessons to meet her students' needs.

She considers how each core lesson approaches prereading, during-reading, and postreading instruction:

- Do the prereading activities develop the knowledge students need to understand the reading?

- Do the prereading activities develop the vocabulary students need to understand the reading?

- Does the lesson include building knowledge about the selection's genre? (Genre often dictates the purpose for reading.)

- Do the number of stopping points in the guided discussion seem excessive or appropriate?

- Are the guided reading questions in the teacher's manual likely to build comprehension or distract students from the ideas in the selection?

- Will the guided reading prompts help students use comprehension strategies?

- Will the postreading activities bring students to a higher level of understanding?

Selecting Texts

Mrs. Richman selects her texts from the student anthology, the core program's leveled books, and the nonfiction books and novels in the school's book room. Whenever possible, these selections tie in with the theme of the unit. It is important that these texts present few decoding problems; students should be able to read them with 90 percent or better accuracy. Since the goal is to develop comprehension, word recognition should not get in the way. Second, the texts she picks are interesting and engaging; comprehension requires some effort, and students are not willing to expend that effort on a boring text. One way to promote interest and engagement is to offer choice. Often Mrs. Richman picks two books, introduces both, and lets students decide between them. She also wants the stories and articles students read to present some challenges and looks for texts with important ideas and themes that give students something to think about. Finally, she wants texts related to the theme of the unit, so that knowledge builds from one selection to the next. Texts that are topically and thematically related enable all students, regardless of their ability, to share in whole-class projects.

Comprehension builds when students read extensively, so Mrs. Richman's text choices often go beyond the core program. For the best readers in the class she moves outside the core program, as early as the middle of first grade, and begins to work with chapter books, novels, and nonfiction trade books. Even average and struggling readers need more than one main anthology selection and one leveled reader per week to promote reading health. She tries to find both challenging and easy chapter books and nonfiction trade books so all readers have a sense of accomplishment.

Planning Guided Discussion

Once Mrs. Richman has selected her texts, she plans the during-reading portions of her guided comprehension lessons. This is difficult work and takes time. She reads each selection twice, first to understand it and again to identify problems that hinder comprehension. She writes instructional notes and guiding questions on Post-its, which she affixes next to the material to which they apply. She also asks her students to read the story or article (or parts of it) twice. The first reading develops comprehension; during the second they can pay attention to the author's use of language, evaluate the material, and make critical judgments. Struggling readers can also focus on decoding problems during the second reading.

To plan successfully:

- Read the selection for your own understanding and enjoyment.
- Read the selection a second time and ask, *What are the big ideas I want my students to acquire by reading this selection?*
- Search for comprehension problems—targets for your questions and probes. They include:
  - Complex pronoun–noun relationships students might not connect.
  - Complex sentences obscuring cause and effect.
  - Ideas or sentences that must be linked to others.
  - Vocabulary and knowledge that must be clarified.
  - Inferences required to understand the text.
  - Required connections with prior knowledge.
- Determine where and how often you will stop and discuss the material:
  - With stories, stop after the setting has been established, after a major character and her problem have been introduced and after an event has played out. Be careful not to break the momentum of the story.

- With nonfiction, stop after a new idea has been introduced and elaborated.

- Also stop anytime the text becomes difficult to understand.

- Frame questions and strategies on Post-its affixed at the point you will use them. They are your lesson plan.

- After the lesson, keep the notes in the text so they're ready to be used again.

Teaching Your Guided Comprehension Lessons

Whether your students are reading the anthology selection, a leveled book, a novel, or a nonfiction trade book, you must engage in prereading activities, guide students' comprehension while they are reading, and solidify their understanding when they have finished. The degree of instruction depends on the skills of your students and the demands of the selection. Good readers need much less direction than struggling readers. (Later in the chapter we offer suggestions for differentiating your instruction.) Let's observe Mrs. Richman in action.

Prereading Activities

Early in the year Mrs. Richman ensures that reading is purposeful by setting a goal for her students, but as the year progresses she helps students set their own purpose. Understanding genre is helpful here, because writers signal their purpose through genre. Mrs. Richman and her students create a genre chart (see Figure 8.1) and continually update it. At first it contains just the headings. As new genres are encountered, Mrs. Richman labels the genre (*realistic fiction, fantasy*), and she and the students explore its characteristics and the purpose for reading it. Students read a few paragraphs from each new selection, examine the pictures or graphics, discuss its genre, use the genre chart to help them set a purpose for reading, and list the selection in the appropriate section of the example column.

Next, Mrs. Richman makes sure critical knowledge is available to the students. Sometimes this means activating knowledge they already have; other times she needs to build new knowledge (see Chapter 7). She teaches the critical vocabulary (see Chapter 6). She briefly discusses the author and his or her work. Sharing other books written by the authors of the core selections motivates students to read beyond the program.

Figure 8.1.   Mrs. Richman's Genre Chart

Genre	Characteristics	Purpose for Reading	Examples
Realistic Fiction	Made-up stories about the here and now; things that could really have happened but didn't	To be entertained and learn a lesson or two about life	*Ramona Quimby, Age 8* (Beverly Cleary) *Poppa's New Pants* (Angela Medearis)
Fantasy	A story set in a make-believe world, with fantastic characters doing superhuman things	To be entertained and perhaps learn a moral lesson	*The Garden of Abdul Gasazi* (Chris Van Allsburg)
Biography	The life story and achievements of an important person written by another person	To be inspired by the achievements of a person's life	

During-Reading Discussions

The best opportunity to guide comprehension is while students are reading. A guided lesson doesn't ask students to use strategies arbitrarily (*Can anyone make an inference or a connection? Who would like to make a prediction?*). Nor is a guided lesson an oral quiz (*Who remembers where Bob and Juan went first?*). Mrs. Richman wants "grand conversations, not gentle inquisitions" (Eeds and Wells 1989). Therefore she asks questions that compel students to put ideas together and make inferences. When questions fail, she models her thinking and coaches students to think as she does. Guidelines from *Questioning the Author* (Beck et al.1997) inform her thinking.

Mrs. Richman always has her students read the story (or a section of it) more than once. During the first reading the students get a basic understanding of the story, focus on characters and what motivates or drives them, the setting, the problem, and the plot (fiction) or the main ideas and the facts that support them (nonfiction). During the second reading they focus on the author's craft. How does his language affect his purpose? How do specific words shape the tone and mood of the story? How do graphics aid comprehension? How might we attack some difficult words? What are some strategies for determining a word's meaning?

THE FIRST READING.   Should the students read the text silently, orally, or chorally? Mrs Richman strives for as much silent reading as possible. Her goal is to build up students' independent reading skills. Echo reading and choral reading emphasize oral performance, not silent comprehension. Round robin reading has many disadvantages, not the least of which is students not paying attention while they wait for their turn (Opitz and Rasinski 2008). Partner reading is a reasonable alternative to reading silently, especially for those students who don't do it well. The goal is to move students as rapidly as possible from reading short pieces of text orally to reading longer texts silently.

Mrs. Richman assembles her group and begins her guided comprehension lesson. The stronger readers, who need less support, come to the group having already read the text, while the weaker students read the text in the small group. Each time Mrs. Richman reaches a stopping point, she:

1. *Asks students to paraphrase.* To get an insight into their comprehension, she asks them to retell the story, giving them the opportunity to put ideas together and demonstrate what they understand and what they have internalized about the selection (the phrase *retelling* works best for younger readers; *paraphrasing* for older students):

   - What is the story/article about?
   - What is the author trying to tell us?
   - What is the author talking about?
   - Who can tell us more?
   - Who can add on to what [name] told us?

2. *Resolves comprehension problems.* If the students' retellings and summaries are incomplete or wrong, she asks questions that will resolve these problems. For a narrative she might ask:

   - Where does the story take place?
   - Who are the main characters and what are their problems?
   - How does [character] try to resolve his [her] problem?
   - How does [character] feel?
   - What will he [she] do next?
   - How does the author let you know that something has changed?
   - How do things look now for [character]?

   For informational text she asks questions like:

   - What is the author writing about? What is the topic?
   - What do you think are his [her] main ideas?

- What facts support his [her] main idea or topic?

- Is that stated clearly?

- How does this connect with what the author has already told us?

3. *Helps students make inferences.* Making inferences is the most important comprehension strategy; it may be the essence of reading. Inferences tie the text ideas
together and link the text to prior knowledge. Research suggests that 70 percent
of comprehension questions or probes should be inferential or require higher-
order thinking (Hansen and Pearson 1983):

- How does [character] feel? (Narrative)

- How would you describe [character]? What kind of person is he [she]?
  (Narrative, character traits)

- What is [character]'s goal? (Narrative, character motives)

- What caused [event] to happen? (Narrative or expository text, cause and
  effect)

- What is the goal of [policy or position]? (Expository text, purpose)

- What seems to be the author's main idea? (Expository text)

Some inferences require links between ideas within the passage:

- Does this make sense with what the author told us before?

- How does this connect to what the author told us before?

- Who or what is the author referring to when he wrote about [event,
  occurrence]?

- How is _____ connected to _____?

Some inferences need to be justified:

- What clues led you to the author's main message?

- What clues led you to determine the character's feelings, motives,
  or traits?

Mrs. Richman applies this type of questioning to eight pages of *Officer Buckle and Gloria*
(Rathmann 1995), a selection in her second-grade core reading program (see Figure 8.2). The
teacher's manual suggests questions for every page of the story, but Mrs. Richman makes a
number of adjustments:

1. She cuts down the number of stopping points in the story in order to maintain flow and enjoyment.

2. She eliminates speculative questions that rely mostly on prior knowledge rather than information in the text. (*How do you think Officer Buckle came up with safety tip number 77? What would happen if you didn't follow this safety tip?*)

3. She ignores suggestions like explaining the role and function of police dogs, which should be done before or after reading the story.

4. She eliminates all questions about decoding words and covers decoding strategies in the second reading of the story.

5. She models a strategy only if students are truly struggling.

She ends up stopping only twice and centers her questions on the most critical ideas: Officer Buckle was a bore while delivering his safety talks; everyone ignored him; his police dog Gloria was extremely entertaining; and Buckle was clueless that the audiences' very enthusiastic responses were because of Gloria's antics, not his presentation. She feels these issues get to the heart of the story.

Figure 8.2. Mrs. Richman's Comprehension Instruction During the First Reading of *Officer Buckle and Gloria*

	Text	Questions and Prompts
Page 1	Officer Buckle knew more safety tips than anyone else in Napville. Every time he thought of a new one, he thumbtacked it to his bulletin board. Safety Tip #77 NEVER stand on a SWIVEL CHAIR	
Page 2	Office Buckle shared his safety tips with the students at Napville School. Nobody ever listened. Sometimes there was snoring.	

(continues)

(continued)

	Text	Questions and Prompts
Page 3	Afterwards, it was business as usual. Mrs. Topple, the principal, took down the welcome banner. "NEVER stand on a SWIVEL CHAIR," said Officer Buckle, but Mrs. Topple didn't hear him.	**Stop 1** What is the story about? Who can summarize it for us? Who can tell us about what Officer Buckle does? What is the principal doing while Officer Buckle is talking? Why do you think the principal didn't hear Officer Buckle?
Pages 3–4	Then one day, Napville's police department bought a police dog named Gloria. When it was time for Office Buckle to give the safety speech at the school Gloria went along. "Children, this is Gloria, "announced Office Buckle. "Gloria obeys my commands. Gloria. SIT!" and Gloria sat.	
Page 5	Officer Buckle gave Safety Tip Number One: "KEEP your SHOELACES TIED!" The children sat up and stared.	
Page 6	Officer Buckle checked to see if Gloria was sitting at attention. She was.	
Pages 7–8	"Safety Tip Number Two," said Officer Buckle. "ALWAYS wipe up spills BEFORE someone SLIPS AND FALLS." The children's eyes popped. Officer Buckle checked on Gloria again. "Good Dog," he said. Officer Buckle thought of a safety tip he had discovered that morning.	**Stop 2** What has happened now in the story? Who can summarize it for us? How would you describe Officer Buckle? What kind of person is he? How do the illustrations help us understand what Gloria is doing? What does the author mean by saying "The children's eyes popped?" Why did their eyes pop?

THE SECOND READING.   During the second reading, Mrs. Richman and her students consider the author's style and use of language, discuss the illustrations, evaluate the story critically, and make connections with other texts. She decides what issues she wants to explore, and asks one of the students to read the related text segment aloud. (This lets students work on their fluency.) Then she poses questions that prod students to wrestle with higher levels of thought and examine the text more deeply:

1. What made Officer Buckle's safety talks so popular?

2. How does Officer Buckle finally figure out why he became so popular? Where in the text does the author let us know this?

3. How do the illustrations help you understand why the kids loved Officer Buckle and Gloria?

4. On page 7 the author capitalizes several words. Why does she do that?

5. Last week when we read *George and Martha* [Marshall 1974] how did we learn about George's dislike of pea soup? This week in *Officer Buckle* how did we learn about his feelings about giving safety talks? Let's compare the techniques of both authors.

6. Who would like to share his favorite part? Why did you pick that part?

7. What makes the students' initial reaction to Officer Buckle so funny?

Postreading Activities

Postreading activities serve a number of purposes. They help students synthesize what they have read and organize the ideas so they can understand and recall them better. They give students the opportunity to evaluate the selection, tell whether they liked it or not, discuss its message, and evaluate the skills of the writer. They also allow students to express a personal response or connection to the text—consider the story or the information in light of their own experience.

Core reading programs provide some but not all of these options. Typically students are asked to summarize or retell what they have read and answer comprehension questions that focus on plot, major ideas, and connections with their experience and with other texts in the program. After that, students move on quickly to skills like fluency, vocabulary, grammar, or writing.

You might begin a discussion by asking students to explain in their own words what the story was about and follow up with evaluative questions: *What was your favorite part?*

Your least favorite part? Why? Read from a page where you really liked how the author described a character or an exciting piece of the action. Or you can ask the students to make connections: *Think of a book or story that has a similar message or covers similar ideas.* A postreading can also involve reteaching. If you discover that students have difficulty summarizing or making inferences, it is important to reteach these skills—but only to the students who need the help.

Avoid repeating activities once students have demonstrated their expertise. Some core reading programs and teachers have students complete a story map for every selection that is read. Story maps help students understand narrative structure. When students can complete a story map easily and successfully, the story map activity has served its purpose; it's time to move on to new and more complex activities. Focus on character development or how setting influences the plot.

Good postreading activities include:

- Creating a graphic representation of the selection (story maps or character maps for fiction, concept maps for nonfiction).

- Creating oral or written summaries of a story or informational article.

- Dramatizing all or a portion of the story or bringing some scene from fiction or history to life.

- Developing an artistic representation of the story (drawings, storyboards, dioramas, collages, posters).

- Writing about the story by comparing and contrasting one character with another or comparing a character in the current story with a character in another story.

- Creating an alternative ending or a "what if" situation. (*What if Officer Buckle figured out what Gloria was doing? What would he do?*)

Differentiating Your Comprehension Instruction

For some children comprehension presents few problems. They bring to the page a large vocabulary and ample background knowledge. This knowledge and solid reasoning skills make comprehension relatively effortless, especially when they are reading fiction and familiar nonfiction. For other students comprehension is difficult and requires a well-articulated instructional plan. You need to be able to differentiate your instruction for strong and weak comprehenders using the tools in a core reading program but often going beyond it.

The last several generations of core programs have attempted to provide tools for differentiating comprehension instruction. Through the 1980s and 1990s, core programs provided reteaching lessons, arguing that additional instruction and practice worksheets would help students who did not pass criterion-referenced tests. Later, the programs added leveled texts for students reading below, on, and above grade level. While this eased the decoding burden for some students, they were reading easier books; it did not solve all the underlying comprehension problems. Few of these attempts at differentiation got to the heart of the problem or considered why the student had difficulty comprehending.

Comprehension Instruction for Struggling Readers

Students have difficulty understanding what they read for several reasons. Some students have not mastered decoding and much of their mental effort still goes to reading the words. When the attention necessary for comprehension is diverted to word recognition, comprehension is frustrating. If an informal reading inventory or a running record indicates that a child is reading with less than 90 percent accuracy on grade-level material, the likely culprit is decoding, not comprehension. Other students have adequate word recognition but poor fluency. Their reading is slow, laborious, and lacks phrasing. It drags them down and prevents them from attending to the meaning. They are not forming words into meaningful phrase units, and comprehension suffers. If decoding and fluency are the source of comprehension difficulty many solutions are available (see Chapters 4 and 5).

However, some children who have adequate decoding and fluency skills still have difficulty comprehending; some educators label these students *word callers* (Cartwright 2010; Dewitz and Dewitz 2003). These students struggle for three likely reasons. Some may lack the vocabulary to understand what they read; they need more vocabulary instruction than the core program provides. Others may have difficulty making connections among ideas in the text and making inferences that connect text ideas to their prior knowledge (Cain, Oakhill, and Bryant 2004). Still others may lack metacognition—they fail to notice when comprehension breaks down and don't know how to repair it.

Students who struggle with comprehension do not fall neatly into one or another of these categories—some weak readers fall into two or even three—but the suggested instructional ideas that follow can be combined. The best way to gain insight into a student's comprehension problem is through an informal reading inventory such as *Qualitative Reading*

Inventory–5 (Leslie and Caldwell 2011). This assessment tool allows you to examine how prior knowledge, strategy use, and metacognition affect students' comprehension. It also allows you to probe students' thinking and determine whether their comprehension is better with narrative or expository text.

VOCABULARY SOLUTIONS.   Comprehension problems stemming from lack of word knowledge are especially common with English language learners and students from low-income families. Make vocabulary the center of your intervention efforts. A core reading program typically introduces eight or ten words a week. We suggest that you double that number and provide some additional direct vocabulary instruction in small groups. The leveled books in the core programs and the trade books you add are good sources for additional vocabulary words.

Remember to select and teach words that are important to the meaning of the story and will have wide general use. Teach new labels (typically found in fictional texts) for known words (*bewildered* for *confused*, *spunky* for *lively*, *delectable* for *tasty*). Words for new concepts in science and social science (*amoeba, meridian, legislature*) require in-depth instruction that prompts students to consider characteristics, examples, and usage. The following instructional strategies can help you boost students' vocabulary:

- *Personal dictionary.* Have students keep a personal dictionary in which they record all new words they are learning, their meanings, synonyms, antonyms, and prefixes and suffixes. Ask them to use their personal dictionary whenever they are writing or reading.

- *Self-selection.* When students are reading independently, tell them to record all words they don't know in their personal dictionary and explore synonyms and antonyms. Once a week have them place these words on the class word wall.

- *Context/dictionary.* Introduce students to new words in a rich context, have them use the context to infer a word's meaning, and then use a dictionary to verify the meaning. Discuss the words with the students and have them try them out orally.

- *Deep processing.* Push students to think more deeply about words. Ask them to classify words from their personal dictionaries and explain their classification. Ask them to answer questions that require knowing word meanings. (*Can you make an appointment for your accident? Yes ___ No ___ Explain why or why not.*) Look at the other activities we suggested in Chapter 6.

CONNECTION SOLUTIONS. Some struggling readers fail to develop a well-integrated internal model of the text. They are unable to connect one sentence and one idea to another or connect the text to their prior knowledge. Inside their head is a collection of bits and pieces, and their internalized version of the story or article lacks an overall connected structure. When struggling readers attempt to retell or summarize a story, they offer only enticing details, not the overall plot. When they paraphrase an informational text they report disjointed facts.

English language learners are likely to have problems making connections because they have yet to master English grammar and vocabulary. Not knowing about pronouns (*he, it, they*) and adjectives (*few, some, many*), they fail to connect one sentence to another. (Remember some adjectives function as pronouns.) Other students fail to make connections because they are not processing the signal words that tie ideas together (*because, since, however*). These interventions are helpful:

- *Pronoun–noun and adjective–noun relationships.* Review the role of pronouns and adjectives. Have students identify, in a series of increasingly complex sentences, the noun a pronoun refers to or an adjective describes. Have them draw lines between the pronouns and their references when reading connected text. Question students about pronoun–noun relationships. Prompt them to tie one sentence or one idea to another.

- *Story mapping and summarizing.* Teach the basic story elements or story grammar (characters, setting, problem, events, solution). Knowing the structure helps students put all the elements in a story together. Have students create story maps (for narratives) and concept maps (for nonfiction) and use them to produce oral and written summaries (see Chapter 7).

- *Questioning.* During reading discussions, ask questions that prompt students to use causal links (*because, since*), lexical links (*some, few, many*), and synonyms (*horse, stallion*) to tie the ideas in a passage together:
  - Who is the author talking about when she uses the word *he* [*she, they*, etc.]?
  - How does that idea connect to what the author already told us?
  - What caused [event or occurrence] to happen?
  - What happened when the character did [action]?

METACOGNITIVE SOLUTIONS. Some students don't notice that what they are reading doesn't make sense (or if they notice, they do little to correct their misunderstanding). Some researchers talk about students having low standards for coherence and don't care that their comprehension is incomplete (Oakhill and Cain 2007). Instructional strategies like reciprocal teaching (Oczkus 2003; Palincsar and Brown 1984) or collaborative strategic reading (Klinger et al. 2004) foster metacognitive insights.

- *Reciprocal teaching.* Students take turns leading the discussion using four comprehension strategies: predicting, questioning, clarifying, and summarizing.

  - Introduce and explain the four strategies.

  - Using a short passage from a longer text, model asking questions, clarifying difficult ideas, summarizing, and making predictions. The teacher is the discussion leader.

  - Ask one of the students to become the discussion leader for the next portion of the text, asking questions, clarifying, summarizing, and make predictions. Provide support as necessary.

  - Have the remaining students take a turn leading the discussion.

- *The "click and clunk" collaborative reading strategy.* Give each student two three-by-five-inch cards, one containing the word *click*, the other, *clunk*. If the paragraph students just read makes sense, they hold up the *click* card, if not they hold up *clunk*. If they hold up *click*, ask them to explain the text. If they hold up *cluck*, have them explore (what didn't make sense?) and solve the problem they encountered.

Comprehension Instruction for Strong Readers

Core reading programs typically provide few resources for your best readers. There are leveled readers for students reading above grade level, but these books are not challenging enough, engaging enough, or long enough to hold the interest of strong readers. Core program worksheets and practice books for above-average readers do not provide the challenges these students need. Indeed they don't need to complete any worksheets at all. As Connor and her colleagues have documented (2009), these students develop their comprehension ability by reading longer texts independently or with a partner and working on more complex projects. Once students are reading significantly above grade level, core reading programs lack the resources to prompt higher levels of achievement.

Children who are ready for chapter books and nonfiction trade books (this can be as early as first grade) should move from core reading programs into the wider world of children's literature. Although they should still participate in whole-class lessons, the bulk of their reading and writing will be done independently and in homogeneous groups. Guidelines for dealing with the best readers in your room include:

- *Spend less time with them.* These students grow when they read independently and work on engaging projects. They need less of your time than struggling readers do (Connor et al. 2009), but they and their parents need to know you have a program that meets their needs. Budget your small-group time accordingly.

- *Have them read chapter books, novels, and nonfiction trade books.* Let them choose from among books you have preselected that are consistent with the theme in the core program.

- *Provide only the strategy instruction they need.* These students know how to comprehend, so teaching them basic strategies is unnecessary. Instead, introduce them to strategies that will take them deeper into books: self-questioning, figurative language, foreshadowing, flashbacks, types of conflict.

- *Skip most if not all workbook activities.*

- *Have them raise their own questions.* Ask students to prepare their own questions about a story or a chapter in a novel for a small-group discussion. (Have your own questions ready to supplement what they leave out.) Teach them Taffy Raphael's (1986) four question types in her question–answer relationship system:

  - *Right-there questions.* The answer is explicit and in the text. (*What kinds of talks did Officer Buckle give?*)

  - *Think-and-search questions.* The answer is in the text but requires comparing and contrasting or integrating information from several paragraphs. (*Compare the children's response to Officer Buckle with their response to Gloria.*)

  - *Author-and-me questions.* The author provides clues, but the answer is in your head. (*How did Officer Buckle figure out he was a bore?*)

  - *On-my-own questions.* The answer is in your head and may require an opinion, a judgment, or a creative response. (*What is a good way to teach children about safety?*)

- *Have them participate in a literature circle.* A literature circle discusses a story, chapter book, or information book with minimal direction from you (Daniels

1996). Each student performs a specific function, or *role*, and the roles rotate each time the groups meets. (See Chapter 5 for a more detailed discussion.)

Extending Your Learning

Reading comprehension instruction is complex. The more you learn about the texts your students will be reading, the better you can assist them:

- Identify core program texts and nonfiction trade books and novels that will build students' knowledge and develop their comprehension ability. Make sure these texts have some meat and are interesting to discuss.
- As grade-level colleagues, select four or five stopping points in a text that lends itself to engaging conversations. Come up with your own questions to raise.
- Do the same for several leveled books in your core programs.
- Create a genre chart to help students set a purpose for reading.

Further Reading

Beck, Isabel, Margaret McKeown, Rebecca Hamilton, and Linda Kucan. 1997. *Questioning the Author*. Newark, DE: International Reading Association.

Cartwright, Kelly. 2010. *Word Callers*. Portsmouth, NH: Heinemann.

Kendal, Juli, and Outey Khuon. 2005. *Making Sense: Small-Group Comprehension Lessons for English Language Learners*. Portland, ME: Stenhouse.

References

Professional Works

Adams, Marilyn, 1990. *Beginning to Read.* Cambridge, MA: MIT Press.

———. 2009. "Decodable Text: Why, When and How?" In *Finding the Right Text*, edited by Elfrieda Hiebert and Misty Sailor. New York: Guilford.

Adams, Marilyn, Barbara Foorman, Ivar Lundberg, and Terri Beeler. 1998. *Phonemic Awareness in Young Children.* Baltimore, MD: Brookes.

Afflerbach, Peter, P. David Pearson, and Scott Paris. 2008. "Clarifying Differences Between Reading Skills and Strategies." *The Reading Teacher* 61 (5): 364–73.

Allington, Richard. 2006. "Fluency: Still Waiting After All These Years." In *What Research Has to Say About Fluency Instruction*, edited by S. Jay Samuels and Alan Farstrup. Newark, DE: International Reading Association.

———. 2009. "If They Don't Read Much . . . 30 Years Later." In *Reading More, Reading Better*, edited by Elfrieda Hiebert. New York: Guilford.

Allington, Richard, and Patricia Cunningham. 2002. *Schools That Work.* Boston: Allyn and Bacon.

Anderson, Richard, and Peter Freebody. 1981. "Vocabulary Knowledge." In *Comprehension and Teaching*, edited by John Guthrie. Newark, DE: International Reading Association.

Anderson, Richard, and William Nagy. 1992. "The Vocabulary Conundrum." *American Educator* 16 (4): 14–18, 44–47.

Anderson, Richard, and P. David Pearson. 1984. "A Schematic-Theoretic View of Basic Processes in Reading Comprehension." In *Handbook of Reading Research*, edited by P. David Pearson, Rebecca Barr, Michael L. Kamil, and Peter Mosenthal. New York: Longman.

Anderson, Richard, Paul Wilson, and Linda Fielding. 1988. "Growth in Reading and How Children Spend Their Time Outside of School." *Reading Research Quarterly* 23 (Summer): 285–303.

Baker, Linda, and Lisa C. Beall. 2009. "Metacognitive Processes and Reading Comprehension." In *Handbook of Research on Reading Comprehension*, edited by Susan Israel and Gerald Duffy. New York: Routledge.

Barr, Rebecca, and Marilyn Sadow. 1989. "Influence of Basal Programs on Fourth-Grade Reading Instruction." *Reading Research Quarterly* 24: 44–71.

Baumann, James, and Kathleen Heubach. 1996. "Do Basal Readers Deskill Teachers? A National Survey of Educators' Use and Opinions of Basals." *Elementary School Journal* 96: 511–26.

Baumann, James, Donna Ware, and Elizabeth Edwards. 2007. "'Bumping into Spicy, Tasty Words That Catch Your Tongue': A Formative Experiment on Vocabulary Instruction." *The Reading Teacher* 62: 108–22.

Bear, Donald, Marcia Invernizzi, Shane Templeton, and Francine Johnston. 2011. *Words Their Way*. 5th ed. Boston: Allyn & Bacon.

Beck, Isabel. 2006. *Making Sense of Phonics*. New York: Guilford.

Beck, Isabel, Margaret McKeown, and Linda Kucan. 2002. *Bringing Words to Life*. New York: Guilford.

Beck, Isabel, Margaret McKeown, and Richard Omanson. 1987. "The Effects and Uses of Diverse Vocabulary Instructional Techniques." In *The Nature of Vocabulary Acquisition*, edited by Margaret McKeown and Mary Curtis. Mahwah, NJ: Lawrence Erlbaum.

Beck, Isabel, Margaret McKeown, Rebecca Hamilton, and Linda Kucan. 1997. *Questioning the Author*. Newark, DE: International Reading Association.

Blevins, Wiley. 2002. *Building Fluency: Lessons and Strategies for Reading Success*. New York: Scholastic.

Block, Cathy Collins, Sheri Parris, Kelly Reed, Cinnamon Whiteley, and Maggie Cleveland. 2009. "Instructional Approaches That Significantly Increase Reading Comprehension." *Journal of Educational Psychology* 101 (2): 262–81.

Bond, Guy, and Robert Dykstra. 1967. "The Cooperative Research Program in First-Grade Reading Instruction." *Reading Research Quarterly* 2 (4): 5–142.

Bradley, Lynn, and Peter Bryant. 1983. "Categorizing Sounds and Learning to Read—A Causal Connection." *Nature* 301: 419–21.

Brenner, Devon, and Elfrieda Hiebert. 2010. "If I Follow the Teachers' Edition, Isn't That Enough? Analyzing Reading Volume in Six Core Reading Programs." *Elementary School Journal* 110 (3): 347–63.

Brown, Rachel, and Peter Dewitz. In press. *Teaching Reading Comprehension*. New York: Guilford.

Brown, Rachel, Michael Pressley, Peggy van Meter, and Ted Schuder. 1996. "A Quasi-Experimental Validation of Transactional Strategy Instruction with Low-Achieving Second-Grade Readers." *Journal of Educational Psychology* 88: 18–37.

Button, Kathryn, Margaret Johnson, and Paige Furgerson. 1996. "Interactive Writing in a Primary Classroom." *The Reading Teacher* 49 (6): 446–54.

Cain, Kate, Jane Oakhill, and Peter Bryant. 2004. "Children's Reading Comprehension Ability: Concurrent Prediction by Working Memory, Verbal Ability, and Component Skills." *Journal of Educational Psychology* 96 (1): 31–42.

Cartwright, Kelly 2010. *Word Callers*. Portsmouth, NH: Heinemann.

Chall, Jeanne S. 1983. *Stages of Reading Development*. New York: McGraw-Hill.

Chall, Jeanne, and James Squire. 1991. "The Publishing Industry and Textbooks." In *Handbook of Reading Research*, vol. 2, edited by Rebecca Barr, Michael Kamil, Peter Mosenthal, and P. David Pearson. New York: Longman.

Chambliss, Marilyn, and Robert Calfee. 1998. *Textbooks for Learning*. Malden, MA: Blackwell.

Clay, Marie. 1993. *Reading Recovery: A Guidebook for Teachers in Training*. Portsmouth, NH: Heinemann.

———. 2006. *An Observation Survey of Early Literacy Achievement*. Rev. 2nd ed. Portsmouth, NH: Heinemann.

Connor, Carol, Frederick Morrison, and Lee Katch. 2004. "Beyond the Reading Wars: Exploring the Effects of Child-Instruction Interaction on Growth in Early Reading." *Scientific Studies of Reading* 8: 305–36.

Connor, Carol, Frederick Morrison, and Phyllis Underwood. 2007. "A Second Chance in Second Grade: The Independent and Cumulative Impact of First- and Second-Grade Reading Instruction and Students' Letter–Word Reading Skill Growth." *Scientific Studies of Reading* 11: 199–234.

Connor, Carol, Lara Jakobsons, Elizabeth Crowe, and Jane Meadows. 2009. "Instruction, Student Engagement, and Reading Skill Growth in Reading First Classrooms." *Elementary School Journal* 109: 221–50.

Connor, Carol, Frederick Morrison, Barry Fishman, Christopher Schatschneide, and Phyllis Underwood. 2007. "Algorithm-Guided Individualized Reading Instruction." *Science* 315: 464–65.

Cunningham, Patricia. 2005. *Phonics They Use: Words for Reading and Writing*. New York: Pearson.

Daniels, Harvey. 1996. *Literature Circles*. Portland, ME: Stenhouse.

Davis, Barbara, Virginia Resta, Laura Davis, and Alexa Camocho. 2001. "Novice Teachers Learn About Literature Circle Through Collaborative Action Research." *Journal of Reading Education* 26: 1–6.

Davis, Frederick. 1944. "Fundamental Factors in Comprehension in Reading." *Psychometrika* 9: 185–97.

Dewitz, Peter, and Pamela Dewitz. 2003. "They Can Read the Words, but They Can't Comprehend: Refining Comprehension Assessment." *The Reading Teacher* 56 (5): 422–35.

Dewitz, Peter, Jennifer Jones, and Susan Leahy. 2009. "Comprehension Strategy Instruction in Core Reading Programs." *Reading Research Quarterly* 44: 102–26.

Dewitz, Peter, Susan Leahy, Jennifer Jones, and Pamela Sullivan. 2010. *The Essential Guide to Selecting and Using Core Reading Programs*. Newark, DE: International Reading Association.

Dole, Janice, Jeffery Nokes, and Dina Drits. 2009. "Cognitive Strategy Instruction." In *Handbook of Research on Reading Comprehension*, edited by Susan Israel and Gerald Duffy. New York: Rutledge.

Dole, Janice, Gerald Duffy, Laura Roehler, and P. David Pearson. 1991. "Moving from the Old to the New: Research on Reading Comprehension Instruction." *Review of Educational Research* 61 (2): 239–64.

Donovan, Carol, Laura Smolkin, and Richard Lomax. 2000. "Beyond the Independent-Level Text: Considering the Reader-Text Match in First Graders' Self-Selections During Recreational Reading." *Reading Psychology* 21: 309–33.

Duffy, Gerald. 2009. *Explaining Reading*. 2d ed. New York: Guilford.

Duffy, Gerald, Laura Roehler, Michael Meloth, Linda Vavus, Cassandra Book, Joyce Putnam, and Roy Wesselman. 1986. "The Relationship Between Explicit Verbal Explanations During Reading Skill Instruction and Student Awareness and Achievement: A Study of Reading Teacher Effects." *Reading Research Quarterly* 21: 237–52.

Duke, Nell, and P. David Pearson. 2002. "Effective Practices for Developing Reading Comprehension." In *What Research Has to Say About Reading Instruction*, 3d ed., edited by A. E. Farstrup and S. J. Samuels, 205–41. Newark, DE: International Reading Association.

Durkin, Delores. 1979. "What Classroom Observations Reveal About Reading Comprehension Instruction." *Reading Research Quarterly* 14 (4): 481–533.

———. 1981. "Reading Comprehension Instruction in Five Basal Reading Series." *Reading Research Quarterly* 16 (4): 515–44.

———. 1984. "Is There a Match Between What Elementary Teachers Do and What Basal Reader Manuals Recommend?" *The Reading Teacher* 37 (8): 734–44.

Eeds, Maryann, and Deborah Wells. 1989. "Grand Conversation: An Exploration of Meaning Construction in Literature Study Groups." *Research in the Teaching of English* 23: 4–29.

Ehri, Linnea. 1996. "Development of the Ability to Read Words." In *Handbook of Reading Research*, vol. 2, edited by Rebecca Barr, Michael Kamil, Peter Mosenthal, and P. David Pearson. New York: Longman.

———. 2005. "Learning to Read Words: Theory, Findings, and Issues." *Scientific Studies in Reading* 9 (2): 167–88.

Fawson, Parker, D. Ray Reutzel, Sylvia Read, John Smith, and Sharon Moore. 2009. "The Influence of Differing the Paths to an Incentive on Third Graders' Reading Achievement and Attitudes." *Reading Psychology* 30 (6): 564–83.

Fisher, Douglas, and Nancy Frey. 2009. *Background Knowledge: The Missing Piece of Comprehension Instruction*. Portsmouth, NH: Heinemann.

Fisher, Douglas, James Flood, Diane Lapp, and Nancy Frey. 2004. "Interactive Read-Alouds: Is There a Common Set of Implementation Practices?" *The Reading Teacher* 58: 8–17.

Fitzpatrick, Jo, Kim Cernek, and Darcy Tom. 2002. *Getting Ready to Read: Independent Phonemic Awareness Centers for Emergent Readers*. Huntington Beach, CA: Creative Teaching Press.

Fountas, Irene, and Gay Su Pinnell. 1996. *Guided Reading: Good First Teaching for All Children*. Portsmouth, NH: Heinemann.

———. 2008. *Benchmark Assessment System*. Portsmouth, NH: Heinemann.

Ganske, Kathy. 2006. *Word Journeys*. New York: Guilford.

Gaskins, Robert, Jennifer Gaskins, and Irene Gaskins. 1991. "A Decoding Program for Poor Readers—And the Rest of the Class, Too." *Language Arts* 68: 213–25.

Good, Roland, and Ruth Kaminski. 2005. *Dynamic Indicators of Basic Early Literacy Skills*. 6th ed. Eugene, OR: Institute for the Development of Educational Achievement.

Graves, Michael. 2006. *The Vocabulary Book*. New York: Teachers College Press.

Graves, Michael, and Bonnie Graves. 2003. *The Scaffolded Reading Experience*. Boston: Christopher-Gordon.

Graves, Michael, Connie Juel, Bonnie Graves, and Peter Dewitz. 2011. *Teaching Reading in the 21st Century*. 5th ed. Boston: Allyn and Bacon.

Guthrie, John, Allan Wigfield, and Kathleen Perencevich. 2004. *Motivating Reading Comprehension: Concept-Oriented Reading Instruction*. Mahwah, NJ: Lawrence Erlbaum.

Guthrie, John, Allan Wigfield, and Clare VonSecker. 2000. "Effects of Integrated Instruction on Motivation and Strategy Use in Reading." *Journal of Educational Psychology* 92 (2): 331–41.

Hall, Gene, and Shirley Hord. 2000. *Implementing Change: Patterns, Principles, and Potholes.* 2d ed. Boston: Allyn & Bacon.

Hansen, Jane, and P. David Pearson. 1983. "An Instructional Study: Improving the Inferential Comprehension of Good and Poor Fourth-Grade Readers." *Journal of Educational Psychology* 75 (6): 821–29.

Hart, Betty, and Todd R. Risley. 1995. *Meaningful Differences in the Everyday Experience of Young American Children.* Baltimore: Brookes.

Hasbrouck, Jan. 2006. *Quick Phonics Screener.* Minneapolis: Read Naturally.

Heath, Shirley Brice. 1983/1996. *Ways with Words: Language, Life, and Work in Communities and Classrooms.* New York: Cambridge University Press.

Hickman, P., S. D. Pollard-Durodola, and S. Vaughn. 2004. "Storybook Reading: Improving Vocabulary and Comprehension for English Language Learners." *The Reading Teacher* 57 (8): 720–30.

Hirsch, E. D. 2011. "Beyond Comprehension: We Have Yet to Adopt a Common Core Curriculum That Builds Knowledge Grade by Grade—But We Need To." *American Educator* (Winter): 30–42.

Hoffman, James, Misty Sailors, Gerald Duffy, and Natasha Beretvas. 2004. "The Effective Elementary Classroom Literacy Environment: Examining the Validity of the TEX-IN3 Observation System." *Journal of Literacy Research* 36 (3): 303–34.

Hoffman, James, Sarah McCarthey, Judy Abbott, Cheryl Christian, Laura Corman, and Catherine Curry. 1994. "So What's New in the New Basals? A Focus on First Grade." *Journal of Reading Behavior* 26 (1): 47–73.

Invernizzi, Marcia, Joanne Meier, and Connie Juel. 2003. *Phonological Awareness Literacy Screening.* Charlottesville: University of Virginia.

Johnson, Dale, and P. David Pearson. 1976. "Skills Management Systems: A Critique." *The Reading Teacher* 29 (8): 757–64.

Juel, Connie, and Cecilia Minden-Cupp. 2000. "Learning to Read Words: Linguistic Units and Instructional Strategies." *Reading Research Quarterly* 35: 458–92.

Juel, Connie, and Diane Roper-Schneider. 1985. "The Influence of Basal Readers on First-Grade Reading." *Reading Research Quarterly* 20 (2): 134–58.

Kendall, Juli, and Outrey Khuon. 2005. *Making Sense: Small-Group Comprehension Lessons for English Language Learners.* Portland, ME: Stenhouse.

Kintsch, Walter. 1998. *Comprehension: A Paradigm for Cognition.* New York: Cambridge University Press.

Kintsch, Walter, and Eileen Kintsch. 2005. "Comprehension." In *Children's Comprehension and Assessment,* edited by Scott Paris and Steven Stahl. Mahwah, NJ: Lawrence Erlbaum.

Klinger, Janette, Sharon Vaughn, Maria Elena Arguelles, Maria Hughes, and Suzette Leftwich. 2004. "Collaborative Strategic Reading: 'Real-World' Lessons from Classroom Teachers." *Remedial and Special Education* 25 (5): 291–302.

Koskinen, Patricia, and Irene Blum. 1986. "Paired Repeated Readings: A Classroom Strategy for Developing Fluency Reading." *The Reading Teacher* 40 (1): 70–75.

Kuhn, Melanie, and Steven Stahl. 2003. "Fluency: A Review of Developmental and Remedial Practices." *Journal of Educational Psychology* 95: 3–22.

LaBerge, David, and S. Jay Samuels. 1974. "Towards a Theory of Automatic Information Processing in Reading." *Cognitive Psychology* 6: 293–323.

Langer, Judith. 1981. "From Theory to Practice: A Prereading Plan." *Journal of Reading* 25 (November): 152–56.

Leinhardt, Gaea, Naomi Zigmond, and William Cooley. 1981. "Reading Instruction and Its Effect." *American Educational Research Journal* 18 (3): 343–61.

Leslie, Lauren, and Joanne Caldwell. 2009. "Formal and Informal Measures of Reading Comprehension." In *Handbook of Research on Reading Comprehension,* edited by Susan Israel and Gerald Duffy. New York: Routledge.

———. 2011. *Qualitative Reading Inventory–5.* Boston: Allyn & Bacon.

Lonigan, Christopher, Chris Schatschneider, Laura Westburg, and the National Early Literacy Panel. 2008. "Identification of Children's Skills and Abilities Linked to Late Outcomes in Reading, Writing, and Spelling." In *Developing Early Literacy: Report of the National Early Literacy Panel.* Louisville, KY: National Center for Family Literacy.

Lovett, Maureen, Karen Steinbach, and Jan Frijters. 2000. "Remediating the Core Deficits of Developmental Reading Disability: A Double-Deficit Perspective." *Journal of Learning Disabilities* 33 (4): 334–58.

Lovett, Maureen, Lea Lacerenza, Susan Borden, Jan Frijters, Karen Steinbach, and Maria De Palma. 2000. "Components of Effective Remediation for Developmental Reading Disabilities: Combining Phonological and Strategy-Based Instruction to Improve Outcomes." *Journal of Educational Psychology* 90: 263–82.

Manning, Maryann, Marta Lewis, and Marsha Lewis. 2010. "Sustained Silent Reading: An Update of the Research." In *Revisiting Silent Reading*, edited by Elfrieda H. Hiebert and D. Ray Reynolds. Newark, DE: International Reading Association.

Marzano, Robert. 2004. *Building Background Knowledge for Academic Achievement*. Alexandria, VA: Association for Curriculum Development and Supervision.

McCarrier, A., I. C. Fountas, and G. S. Pinnell. 1999. *Interactive Writing: How Language and Literacy Come Together*. Portsmouth, NH: Heinemann.

McGill-Franzen, Anne, Courtney Zmach, Katie Solic, and Jacqueline Zeig. 2006. "The Confluency of Two Policy Mandates: Core Reading Programs and Third-Grade Retention in Florida." *Elementary School Journal* 107: 67–91.

McMahon, Susan, and Taffy Raphael. 1997/2007. *The Book Club Connection*. New York: Teachers College Press.

McKenna, Michael, and Steven Stahl. 2003. *Assessment for Reading Instruction*. New York: Guilford.

McKeown, Margaret, Isabel Beck, and Ronette G. Blake. 2009. "Rethinking Reading Comprehension Instruction: A Comparison of Instruction for Strategies and Content Approaches." *Reading Research Quarterly* 44 (3): 218–55.

Miller, Samuel, and Phyllis Blumenfeld. 1993. "Characteristics of Tasks Used for Skill Instruction in Two Basal Reader Series." *Elementary School Journal* 94: 33–47.

Nagy, William, and Patricia Herman. 1987. "Breadth and Depth of Vocabulary Knowledge: Implications for Acquisition and Instruction." In *The Nature of Vocabulary Acquisition*, edited by Margaret McKeown and Mary E. Curtis. Mahwah, NJ: Lawrence Erlbaum.

National Reading Panel. 2000. *Teaching Children to Read: An Evidence-Based Assessment of the Scientific Research Literature on Reading and Its Implications for Reading Instruction.* Bethesda, MD: National Institute of Child Health & Human Development.

Oakhill, Jane, and Roger Beard. 1999. *Reading Development and the Teaching of Reading.* Oxford, UK: Blackwell.

Oakhill, Jane, and Kate Cain. 2007. "Issues of Causality in Children's Reading Comprehension." In *Reading Comprehension Strategies*, edited by Danielle S. McNamara. New York: Lawrence Erlbaum.

O'Connor, Roland, Kathryn Bell, Kristin Harty, Louise Larkin, Sharry Sackor, and Naomi Zigmond. 2002. "Teaching Reading to Poor Readers in the Intermediate Grades: A Comparison of Text Difficulty." *Journal of Educational Psychology* 94: 474–85.

Oczkus, Lori. 2003. *Reciprocal Teaching at Work.* Newark, DE: International Reading Association.

Ogle, Donna. 1986. "K-W-L: A Teaching Model That Develops Active Reading of Expository Text." *The Reading Teacher* 39 (6): 564–70.

Opitz, Michael, and Timothy Rasinski. 2008. *Good-bye Round Robin.* 2d ed. Portsmouth, NH: Heinemann.

O'Reilly, Tenaha, and Danielle McNamara. 2007. "The Impact of Science Knowledge, Reading Skill and Reading Strategy Knowledge on More Traditional 'High Stakes' Measures of High School Students' Science Achievement." *American Educational Research Journal* 44 (1): 161–96.

Osborn, Jean. 1984. "The Purposes, Uses, and Contents of Workbooks and Some Guidelines for Publishers." In *Learning to Read in American Schools*, edited by Richard C. Anderson, Jean Osborn, and Robert Tierney. Mahwah, NJ: Lawrence Erlbaum.

Palinscar, Annemarie, and Anne L. Brown. 1984. "Reciprocal Teaching of Comprehension Fostering and Monitoring Activities." *Cognition and Instruction* 1: 117–75.

Paris, Scott, and Ellen Hamilton. 2009. "The Development of Children's Reading Comprehension." In *Handbook of Research on Reading Comprehension*, edited by Susan Israel and Gerald Duffy. New York: Routledge.

Paris, Scott, and James Hoffman. 2004. "Reading Assessment in Kindergarten: Findings from the Center for Early Reading Achievement." *Elementary School Journal* 105 (2): 119–218.

Pearson, P. David, and Meg Gallagher. 1983. "The Instruction of Reading Comprehension." *Contemporary Educational Psychology* 8: 317–44.

Pearson, P. David, and Dale Johnson. 1978. *Teaching Reading Comprehension*. New York: Holt Rinehart & Winston.

Perfetti, Charles A. *Reading Ability*. 1985. New York: Oxford University Press.

Piasta, Shyne, Carol Connor, Barry Fishman, and Frederick Morrison. 2009. "Teacher's Knowledge of Literacy Concepts, Classroom Practices, and Student Reading Growth." *Scientific Studies of Reading* 13 (3): 224–48.

Pressley, Michael. 2006. *Reading Instruction That Works: The Case for Balanced Teaching*. 3d ed. New York: Guilford.

Pressley, Michael, Ruth Wharton-McDonald, Lisa M. Raphael, Kristen Bogner, and Alysia Roehig. 2002. "Exemplary First-Grade Teaching." In *Teaching Reading: Effective Schools, Accomplished Teachers*, edited by Barbara Taylor and P. David Pearson. Mahwah, NJ: Lawrence Erlbaum.

RAND Reading Study Group. 2002. *Reading for Understanding: Toward an R & D Program in Reading Comprehension*. Santa Monica, CA: RAND.

Raphael, Taffy. 1986. "Teaching Question–Answer Relationships, Revisited." *The Reading Teacher* 39 (6): 516–22.

Rasinski, Timothy. 2006. "A Brief History of Reading Fluency." In *What Research Has to Say About Fluency Instruction*, edited by S. Jay Samuels and Alan E. Farstrup. Newark, DE: International Reading Association.

———. 2010. *The Fluent Reader: Oral and Silent Reading Strategies for Building Fluency, Word Recognition, and Comprehension*. 2d ed. New York: Scholastic.

Reutzel, D. Ray, John Smith, and Parker Fawson. 2005. "An Evaluation of Two Approaches for Teaching Reading Comprehension Strategies in the Primary Years Using Science Informational Text." *Early Childhood Research Quarterly* 20 (3): 276–305.

Reutzel, D. Ray, Cindy Jones, Parker Fawson, and John Smith. 2008. "Scaffolded Silent Reading: A Complement to Guided Repeated Oral Reading That Works!" *The Reading Teacher* 62 (3): 194–207.

Rosenshine, Barak, and Carla Meister. 1994. "Reciprocal Teaching: A Review of the Research." *Review of Educational Research* 64 (4): 479–530.

Rosenshine, Barak, and Robert Stevens. 1986. "Teaching Functions." In *Handbook of Research on Teaching*, edited by Melvin Wittrock. New York: Macmillan.

Samuels, S. Jay. 1979. "The Method of Repeated Readings." *The Reading Teacher* 32 (4): 403–408.

Santoro, Lana E., David Chard, Lisa Howard, and Scott K. Baker. 2008. "Making the *Very* Most of Classroom Read-Alouds to Promote Comprehension and Vocabulary." *The Reading Teacher* 61 (5): 396–408.

Scanlon, Donna, and Kimberly L. Anderson. 2010. "Using the Interactive Strategies Approach to Prevent Reading Difficulties." In *Successful Approaches to RTI*, edited by Marjorie Y. Lipson and Karen Wixon. Newark, DE: International Reading Association.

Shankweiler, Donald, and Stephen Crain. 2004. "Language Mechanism and Reading Disorder: A Modular Approach." *Cognition* 24: 139–68.

Shapiro, Amy. 2004. "How Including Prior Knowledge as a Subject Variable May Change Outcomes of Learning Research." *American Educational Research Journal* 41 (1): 159–89.

Share, David L. 1995. "Phonological Recoding and Self-Teaching: Sine Qua Non of Reading Acquisition." *Cognition* 55: 151–218.

———. 2004. "Knowing Letter Names and Learning Letter Sounds: A Causal Connection." *Journal of Experimental Child Psychology* 88 (3): 213–33.

Shepard, Lori. 2010. "What the Marketplace Has Brought Us: Item-by-Item Teaching with Little Instructional Insight." *Peabody Journal of Education* 85 (2): 175–89.

Simmons, Deborah, and Edward Kame'enui. 2003. "A Consumer's Guide to Evaluating a Core Reading Program Grades K–3." Eugene: University of Oregon Center on Teaching and Learning. Retrieved January 11, 2009, from http://reading.uoregon.edu/cia/curricula /con_guide.php.

Smith, Nila B. 1986. *American Reading Instruction*. Newark, DE. International Reading Association.

Snow, Catherine, and Connie Juel. 2005. "Teaching Children to Read: What Do We Know About How to Do It." In *The Science of Reading: A Handbook*, edited by Margaret J. Snowling and Charles Hulme. Oxford, UK: Blackwell.

Stahl, Steven. 2001. "Teaching Phonics and Phonological Awareness." In *Handbook of Early Literacy Research*, edited by Susan B. Neuman and David K. Dickinson. New York: Guilford.

Stahl, Steven, and Kathleen Heubach. 2005. "Fluency-Oriented Reading Instruction." *Journal of Literacy Research* 37: 25–60.

Stahl, Steven, and Bruce Murray. 1998. "Issues Involved in Defining Phonological Awareness and Its Relation to Early Reading." In *Word Recognition in Beginning Literacy*, edited by James Metsal and Linnea Ehri. Mahwah, NJ: Lawrence Erlbaum.

Taylor, Barbara, and P. David Pearson. 2005. "Using Study Groups and Reading Assessment Data to Improve Reading Instruction Within a School." In *Children's Comprehension and Assessment*, edited by Scott Paris and Steven Stahl. Mahwah, NJ: Lawrence Erlbaum.

Taylor, Barbara, P. David Pearson, Kathleen Clark, and Sharon Walpole. 2000. "Effective School and Accomplished Teachers: Lessons About Primary-Grade Reading Instruction in Low-Income Schools." *Elementary School Journal* 101 (2): 121–65.

Texas Educational Agency. 1998. *Texas Primary Reading Inventory*. Austin: Texas Educational Agency.

Thomas B. Fordham Institute. 2004. *The Mad, Mad World of Textbook Adoption*. Foreword by Chester E. Finn Jr., introduction by Diane Ravitch. New York: Thomas B. Fordham Institute.

Tunmer, William, and James Chapman. 2006. "Metalinguistic Abilities, Phonological Recoding Skills, and the Use of Sentence Context in Beginning Reading Development: A Longitudinal Study." In *Handbook of Orthography and Literacy*, edited by R. Malt Joshi and P. G. Aaron. Mahwah, NJ: Lawrence Erlbaum.

Tunmer, William, and Tom Nicholson. 2011. "The Development and Teaching of Word Recognition Skills." *In Handbook of Reading Research*, vol. 4, edited by Michael Kamil, P. David Pearson, Elizabeth B. Moje, and Peter Afflerbach. New York: Routledge.

Tunmer, William, James Chapman, and Jane Prochnow. 2006. "Literate Cultural Capital at School Entry Predict Later Reading Achievement: A Seven Year Longitudinal Study." *New Zealand Journal of Educational Studies* 41: 183–204.

Van den Broek, Paul, and Kathleen Kremer. 2000. "The Mind in Action: What It Means to Comprehend During Reading." In *Reading for Meaning*, edited by Barbara Taylor, Michael Graves, and Paul Van Den Broek. Newark, DE: International Reading Association.

Waite, Michele. 2005. Personal Communication.

Walpole, Sharon, and Michael McKenna. 2005. *Differentiated Reading Instruction*. New York: Guilford.

Walsh, Kate. 2003. "Basal Readers: The Opportunity to Build the Knowledge That Propels Comprehension." *American Educator* 27 (1): 24–27.

West. 1953. *A General Service List of English Words*. Retrieved from http://jbauman.com/aboutgsl.html on 6/15/2012.

Wilkinson, Ian A., and Eun Hye Son. 2011. "A Dialogic Turn in Research on Learning and Teaching to Comprehend." In *Handbook of Reading Research*, vol. 4, edited by Michael L.Kamil, P. David Pearson, Elizabeth B. Moje, and Peter Afflerbach. New York: Routledge.

Willingham, Daniel. 2007. "The Usefulness of Brief Instruction in Reading Comprehension Strategies." *American Educator* 31 (4): 39–50.

Wood, Karen. 1984. "Probable Passage: A Writing Strategy." *The Reading Teacher* 37 (8): 496–99.

Yopp, Hallie K., and Harry Singer. 1995. "A Test of Assessing Phonemic Awareness in Young Children." *The Reading Teacher* 49 (10): 20–29.

Children's Literature

Aliki. 1989. *My Five Senses*. New York: HarperCollins.

Allard, Harry, and James Marshall. 1985. *Miss Nelson Is Missing*. New York: Sandpiper.

———. 1986. *Miss Nelson Is Back*. New York: Sandpiper.

Auch, Mary Jane. 2003. *The Princess and the Pizza*. New York: Holiday House.

Base, Graham. 1987. *Animalia*. New York: Harry N. Abrams.

Berger, Melvin. 1992. *Discovering Mars*. New York: Scholastic.

Cowley, Joy. 1996. *Gracias, the Thanksgiving Turkey*. New York: Scholastic.

Cronin, Doreen. 2000. *Click Clack Moo: Cows That Type*. New York: Simon & Schuster.

Danneberg, Julie. 2000. *First Day Jitters*. Watertown, MA: Charlesbridge.

Davidson, Margaret. 1996. *Balto, the Dog Who Saved Nome*. New York: Scholastic.

dePaola, Tomie. 1978. *Pancakes for Breakfast*. Orlando, FL: Harcourt Brace.

Driscoll, Michael. 2003. *A Child's Introduction to Poetry*. New York: Black Dog & Leventhal.

Falwell, Catherine. 1998. *Word Wizard*. New York: Clarion.

Floca, Brian. 2009. *Moonshot: The Flight of Apollo 11*. New York: Atheneum.

Gibbons, Gail. 1993. *From Seed to Plant*. New York: Holiday House.

———. 2000. *The Planets*. New York: Holiday House.

Gwynne, Fred. 1988. *A Little Pigeon Toad*. New York: Simon & Schuster.

Hakim, Joy. 2007. *A History of US*. New York: Oxford University Press.

Henkes, Kevin. 2000. *Wemberly Worried*. New York: HarperCollins.

Hoban, Russell. 1995. *Bread and Jam for Francis*. New York: HarperFestival.

Hurd, Edith Thacher. 2000. *Starfish*. New York: HarperCollins.

Johnson, Bonnie von Hoff. 1999. *Wordworks: Exploring Language Play*. Golden, CO: Fulcrum Publishing.

Kinney, Jeff. 2007. *Diary of a Wimpy Kid*. New York: Amulet Books/Abrams.

Kurtz, Joan. 1998. "My Father Never Takes Me Fishing." *Highlights for Children* 53 (6): 38.

Lederer, Richard. 2001. *The Circus of Words: Acrobatic Anagrams, Parading Palindromes, Wonderful Words on a Wire, and More Lively Letter Play*. Chicago: Chicago Review Press.

Lin, Grace. 2009. *Where the Mountain Meets the Moon*. Boston: Little, Brown.

Lionni, Leo. 1969. *Swimmy*. New York: Dragonfly.

———. 1973. *Alexander and the Wind-Up Mouse*. New York: Dragonfly.

MacLachlan, Patricia. 1985. *Sarah, Plain and Tall*. New York: HarperCollins.

Marshall, James. 1974. *George and Martha*. New York: Sandpiper.

Martin, Bill, and Eric Carle. 2010. *Brown Bear, Brown Bear, What Do You See?* New York: Henry Holt.

McGovern, Ann. 1993. *The Pilgrims' First Thanksgiving*. New York: Scholastic.

Minarik, Else Holmelund. 1957. *Little Bear*. New York: Harper Trophy.

Park, Barbara. 2001. *Junie B. Jones*. First boxed set. New York: Random House.

———. 2002. *Scranimals*. New York: Greenwillow.

Polacco, Patricia. 1997. *Thunder Cake*. New York: Puffin.

Posell, Elsa. 1982. *Whales and Other Sea Mammals*. Chicago: Children's Press.

Prelutsky, Jack. 1984. *The New Kid on the Block*. New York: William Morrow.

Rand, Ann, and Paul Rand. 2006. *Sparkle and Spin: A Book About Words*. San Francisco: Chronicle Books.

Rathmann, Peggy. 1995. *Officer Buckle and Gloria*. New York: Putnam.

Rotner, Shelley. 1996. *Hold the Anchovies!* New York: Orchard Books.

Ryan, Pam Muñoz. 1999. *Amelia and Eleanor Go for a Ride*. New York: Scholastic.

Rylant, Cynthia. 1994. *Mr. Putter and Tabby Pour the Tea*. New York: Sandpiper.

Silverstein, Shel. 1974. *Where the Sidewalk Ends*. New York: Harper & Row.

———. 1981. *A Light in the Attic*. New York: Harper & Row.

Schenk de Regniers, B., M. White, E. Moore, and J. Carr, eds. 1988. *Sing a Song of Popcorn: Every Child's Book of Poems*. New York: Scholastic.

Steig, William. 1982. *Doctor De Soto*. New York: Farrar, Straus & Giroux.

Waber, Bernard. 1975. *Ira Sleeps Over*. New York: Sandpiper.

White. E. B. 2001. *Charlotte's Web*. New York: HarperCollins.